I Mor

16609 Dee

D0330565

MASTER·STROKES

The Short Game

**Hundreds of Proven Lessons for Shaving
Strokes Off Your Score from 100 Yards In**

By
Phil Franké

RUNNING PRESS
PHILADELPHIA · LONDON

© 2012 by Phil Franké
Distributed by King Features Syndicate

All rights reserved under the Pan-American and International Copyright Conventions

Printed in China

This book may not be reproduced in whole or in part, in any form or by any means, electronic or mechanical, including photocopying, recording, or by any information storage and retrieval system now known or hereafter invented, without written permission from the publisher.

Books published by Running Press are available at special discounts for bulk purchases in the United States by corporations, institutions, and other organizations. For more information, please contact the Special Markets Department at the Perseus Books Group, 2300 Chestnut Street, Suite 200, Philadelphia, PA 19103, or call (800) 810-4145, ext. 5000,
or e-mail special.markets@perseusbooks.com.

9 8 7 6 5 4 3 2 1
Digit on the right indicates the number of this printing
Library of Congress Control Number: 2011925149

ISBN 978-0-7624-4397-0

Interior illustrations: Phil Franké
Designer: Matthew Goodman
Editor: Greg Jones
Typography: Lucida, and Franklin Gothic

Running Press Book Publishers
2300 Chestnut Street
Philadelphia, PA 19103-4371

Visit us on the web!
www.runningpress.com

CONTENTS

YAK YAK YAK

SECTION 5:
Strategy . . .164

SECTION 6:
Swing Basics . . .197

SECTION 7:
Short Irons . . .240

SECTION 8:
Pitching . . .258

Introduction

Released in 2003, the original *Master Strokes* book represented perhaps the most comprehensive anthology of golf lessons ever published. It presented hundreds of lessons covering everything from teeing off to putting out. The book's wisdom and user-friendly format made it a big hit with golfers looking to improve their games by reading brief, simple, illustrated tips, and then applying them on the practice range and golf course.

But as anyone who has ever played the game of golf knows, you can never get enough instruction and practice on area in particular—the short game. While short-game shots make up only a small fraction of the total distance covered by a player in a round, they add up to about half his or her total shots on the scorecard, often more. Many of those shots are needlessly wasted due to a lack of knowledge, practice, discipline, strategy, or technique.

With its hundreds of short-game lessons covering everything from short irons to short putts, *Master Strokes: The Short Game* will help you trim a sizable number of strokes off your handicap.

Because it favors discipline and discretion over strength and flexibility, the short game offers senior golfers a particularly good opportunity to keep competing with younger players and continue to enjoy playing golf.

For the purpose of this book, we defined the short game as shots from full-swing short irons, like the 8-iron, to "gimme" putts—and everything in between. The book's 401 tips are divided into 12 sections that take you from preseason preparation, to practice drills, to swing basics, to typical short-game situations, to tricky conditions, to just off the green, to onto the putting green, and into the hole. Each tip addresses a particular aspect of the swing or a particular short-game scenario, so that readers can flip through the book and find the tips that focus on their problem areas. Due to their importance, some aspects of the swing and short game are discussed in multiple tips, because the same tip doesn't always help two different golfers facing the same problem.

The book's structure also makes it easy for readers to consider the details of an individual aspect of the game, and then apply the lessons outlined in a tip through practice—an approach that often proves most effective in helping players improve in maybe the world's most complex, challenging, and rewarding individual sport.

We hope you enjoy *Master Strokes: The Short Game*, and that it increases your understanding and appreciation of the game of golf, as well as your ability to play it well.

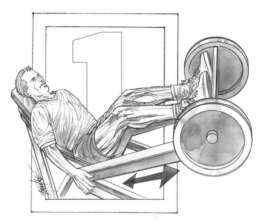

SECTION 1:
Training & Exercise

A good round of golf starts a long time before you step onto the first tee. Not only do you need to stretch and warm up in the minutes leading up to teeing off, you need to maintain and increase your fitness in the months leading up to the start of golf season. Here are a series of exercises that target muscles and movements vital to your golf swing and success on the course.

CONTENTS

MASTER·STROKES

Sttrreettcchh!

Most golfers know that a brief stretching and warmup routine is always needed to help get the round off to a good start. So when it's cold and/or windy at the end of your season, you need to allow more time for a longer warmup. This is even more important for seniors with less flexibility who are already tight and stiff. It's critical to add two to three extra minutes of stretching before you go near the practice tee. Once there, hit 30 balls rather than 20, nice and easy – keep your swing simple. Focus on a slow, rhythmic tempo. This little extra effort to get loose will pay off and reduce your chances of injury. Last thought: Dress a little warmer, but use thin, loose layers that will allow you to move and that you can peel off as you get hot.

Less warmup

100
80
60
40
20

More warmup

Gain Some Weight In The Offseason

It is always important to keep your "golf muscles" in shape. This is even more necessary during the offseason.

A great way to help you do this is swinging a weighted club every day. Take an old driver or fairway wood and add a weighted "doughnut" to it. Believe it or not, adding 6 or 8 ounces to the neck of the club is all you need.

Create a routine of making 50 slow, relaxed swings per day with the weighted club. It will take less than 10 minutes. This program will keep the muscles of your back limber and add surprising strength to your hands and forearms. Result: You'll stay in great shape swinging the club during the offseason, you'll be swinging the club effortlessly when you start the new season, and, of course, this will help you avoid injury.

x50

30 OZ.

MASTER·STROKES

A Good Reason For Offseason

Most golfers across America have a definite "offseason" during the winter months. Putting the clubs away stinks, but this shouldn't be wasted time. The offseason is an opportunity to revitalize your game by dedicating yourself to an offseason exercise regimen. As you age, off-season exercise is needed just to maintain your game at its current level. Of course, check with your doctor before you start any exercise program. Your main fitness goals should be building leg strength, improving abdominal muscles and increasing overall flexibility. When you tee it up early next spring, you'll be ready. With added strength and flexibility, you'll feel better and play better. Being in game shape also will help lower the chances of an early-season injury that could nag you all year long.

Keep Your Legs This Winter

Many athletic moves – for example, pitching a baseball or driving a football over the goal line – require leg power. The full golf swing, particularly the tee shot, also generates most of its power from the lower body or upper legs. The largest muscles, those of the thighs and hips, need the most attention. The golfer who makes an effort to maintain and build upper-leg strength will, over time, gain a tremendous advantage in carrying his or her shots as far as possible. Consult with a trainer or do your own research to learn what exercises and equipment would benefit your upper legs the most. If you commit to an off-season leg-strengthening program, you'll give your power game a big boost next spring.

MASTER·STROKES

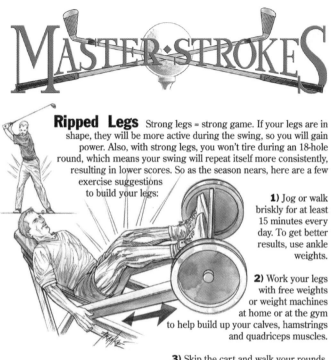

Ripped Legs Strong legs = strong game. If your legs are in shape, they will be more active during the swing, so you will gain power. Also, with strong legs, you won't tire during an 18-hole round, which means your swing will repeat itself more consistently, resulting in lower scores. So as the season nears, here are a few exercise suggestions to build your legs:

1) Jog or walk briskly for at least 15 minutes every day. To get better results, use ankle weights.

2) Work your legs with free weights or weight machines at home or at the gym to help build up your calves, hamstrings and quadriceps muscles.

3) Skip the cart and walk your rounds. Then *"let it rip"* this spring.

Section 1:

Get A Leg Up This Winter

It's a good idea for golfers to strengthen their legs during the offseason. A strong leg base is critical to having a balanced, powerful swing. These two exercises with ankle weights (2 to 5 pounds each) will help. To strengthen your hamstrings, lie on your stomach on a bench. Slowly lift your feet until your legs are pointing straight up. Lower slowly to the starting position and repeat 10 times. To build up your quadriceps, sit in a chair, slowly lift your feet until your legs are parallel to the ground, lower and repeat 10 times. You will have some extra spring in your step next spring, and your strengthened legs will pay off in the more powerful, accurate shots you hit.

MASTER·STROKES

AB-solutely

Many amateur golfers are unaware of the importance of a strong stomach (abdominal muscles) in relation to their golf swings. Strong abdominal muscles are necessary to help you turn fully away in your backswing, and back down through the ball to generate more power. Here's a simple everyday – and especially offseason – exercise to help: the basic stomach crunch. Lie on your back with your feet flat on the floor and your knees bent. Extend your arms, slightly lifting your head and shoulders up from the floor (make sure to keep your head, neck and back straight so as not to strain yourself). As you do this, reach both hands just above and to the left of your left knee. You should feel a tightening of your abs. Back down slowly, then lift again to the right of your right knee. Do sets of 10 per day, gradually increasing the number. Always take it easy with sit-ups, being careful not to hurt your back. There is a wide variety of abdominal crunches, so you should research the one that's right for you.

MASTER·STROKES

Winter Back Maintenance

One thing for sure: The golf swing is not back-friendly. A full swing requires a lot of torque pressure. Add in that many golfers already have some sort of back issue. It's smart to use the offseason to strengthen your back for the coming spring.

Here's a great back exercise. Lie on your stomach with arms stretched above you as shown. Slowly raise one arm and the opposite leg several inches off the ground. Hold them there for a count of five. Lower both, then raise the other arm and opposing leg, again holding for a count of five. Repeat several times. Gradually increase your reps as you do this exercise several times a week. Your back will be "golf-ready" and less susceptible to injury next season.

On The Back Stretch

The game of golf and your back are not a very good match. The twisting that turning through a golf swing requires can easily injure your back. Thinking that you can run up to the first tee and start swinging for the fences without stretching is foolish. You can't possibly swing your best without being loose. You must always spend five to 10 minutes on a stretching routine before you go out on the course or driving range. You should pay most attention to your lower back, because this area is the most prone to injury. Only after you have stretched should you hit 15 to 20 easy warm-up shots on the practice tee. Now you can tee off. The results will be a freer, faster swing and a greatly reduced chance of injury. It's nonnegotiable.

Back Up Your Back!

"Ouch! My aching back!" Unfortunately, it's a sentence heard too often from many amateur golfers. Winter is a great time for all golfers to strengthen their backs so we don't hear these complaints next season. Here are two good back exercises for your workout at the gym or at home if you have your own equipment. Of course, check with your doctor. 1) Seated Row: While sitting upright, grasp the handle with both hands and pull toward you. The motion is as if you're rowing a boat; this works the upper back muscles. 2) Back Extension: From a sitting position, push backward against the resistance as far as you can; this strengthens the sensitive lower back. Find the correct weight that allows you to do 12 to 15 reps without straining. When the warm weather returns, enjoy getting "back" into the game.

SEATED ROW →

Training & Exercise

Get Back To Your Backswing

Over time, many golfers get away from using their entire body while making their backswing. They revert to using just their arms. This is a cause of lost power. Here's an offseason drill to re-enforce a full backswing. Stand at address and pretend you're holding a large ball. Without moving your feet, turn to your right, as if you were handing the ball to someone to the side and slightly behind you. Make sure to turn fully, so your sternum is facing the person taking the handoff. Practice this move often, then incorporate this move into your swing on the practice range, and finally on the course. This spring, you will be back to hitting solid shots that will fly higher and longer.

Be Hip This Winter

Adding strength and flexibility in your hips during the cold winter months will provide a noticeable difference in your power game. Here's a simple stretch that you can do right at home: Kneel on your right knee, with your left foot flat on the floor. Your left foot should be extended forward so that you are in a "lunge" position, which will give you a stretching sensation through the right hip. Hold a club with both hands, your arms extended in front of you. Slowly turn to your right as far as you can while keeping your lower body stable. Hold for a count of 10, then return. Repeat several times. Then switch legs, with your right foot extended out flat on the floor, to stretch your left hip. Again turn your upper body, this time to the left. Hold for a 10 count and repeat several times. Your powerful shots will be very "hip" next spring.

23

Turn That Trim Torso

Listen, believe it or not, this stretching exercise can trim your midsection (love handles), making you a hottie and turning on your game. You will increase your flexibility, allowing you to turn away and through the ball better, resulting in more powerful shots. Find an object weighing 15 to 20 pounds – maybe a medicine ball or a sack of something – and hold it in both arms in front of you. Now turn your torso slowly to the right as far as you can go (be careful not to hurt yourself by pulling a muscle – this is a gradual exercise). Return to center, hold, then slowly turn your torso to the left. Repeat this stretching exercise 20 times a day. You will be surprised how much elasticity you can gain back in a short period of time, in addition to trimming down your waist.

Shoulder Pivot

A shoulder pivot is essential in every golfer's swing for several reasons. First, in order to get distance out of your shots, you must have a range of motion, which you might have lost, that gives you a degree of windup so that you can release power into your swing. Second, a shoulder pivot, when made consistently, can benefit the golfer by providing distance that is reliable. In other words, your distance is not off and on. It is important to keep this range of motion through drills and stretching to maintain flexibility. The tighter your muscles are, the shorter they become, which means the risk of injury is greater and the loss of distance is prevalent. So keep moving to help restore and maintain flexibility for better golf.

Training & Exercise

Good Old Shoulders

Years of playing golf put a
lot of wear and tear on your
front (left) shoulder. The
shoulder can become
weak and make it
painful to play. Here are
two exercises to add back
strength and mobility.

1) Stand facing a wall at
arm's length. Walk
the hand connected to
your injured shoulder up
the wall, wiggling your
fingers as far as you can
reach. Repeat several
times.

2) Take a light weight
(2 to 5 pounds) in the
same hand and lean
over, keeping balance
with your other hand on a

desk or table. Make small, clockwise circular movements with
your hand. Gradually make the circles larger. Slow to a stop, then
make circles in the opposite direction. Repeat several times.

MASTER·STROKES

Strong Hand!

Golfers must work at maintaining their hand strength. Strong hands and wrists are a big advantage out on the golf course. Difficult lies such as deep, snarly rough can slow down and even stop the clubhead at impact, snuffing out the shot. To overcome this, you need to work out. Get yourself one of those springlike hand and wrist exercisers, and keep it handy. Work with it often, making sure to use both hands. It's something you can do while you're waiting around. Like drops of water adding up, a little working out of your hands each day will pay amazing dividends. Strong hands and wrists will give you more control in tough situations and help keep you playing young.

Training & Exercise

Put The Squeeze On!

Gary Player has been a great golfer during his career, including his senior years. He was certainly ahead of his time in regard to physical fitness and how it relates to golf. At any age, it is critical for you to take advantage of any beneficial exercise that would help maintain or restore lost game. Here's one that is both incredibly simple and also incredibly effective. Simply squeeze an old tennis ball for 10 minutes a day with each hand. This simple, quick exercise will give you much-needed hand, forearm, wrist and finger strength. This will lead to more power in your golf swing. Make certain to work the fingers, even the pinkies, on each hand. And pay special attention to the weaker hand, working it out a bit harder.

EACH HAND 10 MIN.

Section 1:

Strong-Arm Tactics

Through the years, many golfers lose strength in their hands and forearms. The "offseason" is an excellent opportunity to build yourself back physically. Try this indoor hand/arm exercise. Get a 5-pound barbell or hand weight and a short, round bar or section of an old broom handle. Tie a 4-foot rope securely to both the bar and weight. Hold the bar out with the weight hanging down in front of you at shoulder height. Using both hands, wind the weight up all the way to the top, then slowly wind it back down. To start out, do this three times a day, then gradually increase the number of reps. After a few weeks, you'll greatly improve your hand and forearm strength. Back out on the course, your newfound strength will increase your power, bringing back some lost distance. Also, your club won't turn as much in your strong hands on mishits, and you'll be able to power your clubhead through the rough. Good deal!

Training & Exercise

SECTION 2:
Equipment

You can't get any job done without the proper tools, and that includes completing a good round of golf. These tips will help you play the game well by employing the right clubs, grips, balls, clothing, and other items critical to a good round of golf.

CONTENTS

Get Off On The Right Foot

Metal spikes are long gone, replaced by soft spikes (rubber or plastic). They are much less damaging to the greens and tee boxes, which is good for the course, but be aware: These soft spikes wear down rather quickly. Playing with poor traction can really hurt your game. A solid base is a must for good balance during the swing. Without it, you'll have no chance to make accurate, consistent contact. Replace your old, worn-out spikes to start the season off on the right foot.

MASTER·STROKES

Lighten Up

Many players tend to wear heavier clothing than most when it's cold out.

It's a comfort thing. They think it's perfectly OK to wear that bulky sweater they got from their Aunt Tilly because it's so warm and fuzzy. Actually, NOT! Amateurs especially don't need any help in restricting their already-limited swing. You won't see the better players wearing clothing that would restrict their golf swing in any way. Fortunately, they don't have to. There are great high-tech, multithin layered fabrics that will keep you warm, let your body breathe and not get in the way of your swinging freely. So chill out with the heavy, bulky outerwear. Stay light, loose and warm.

THIN LAYERS

MASTER·STROKES

Rain Ready

Playing golf is great; playing golf in the rain can be miserable. You can avoid misery by being "rain ready." Always have a breathable rain suit in your bag and waterproof golf shoes to combat bad-luck rainy days or sudden showers. Now that

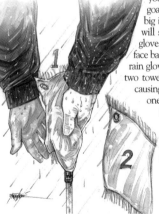

you'll be reasonably comfortable, your next goal is to play as well as can be expected. The big issue here is having a good grip. Your club will slip during your swing with a wet grip or glove, making it impossible to deliver the club-face back to square at impact. What you need is a rain glove that is rubberized (grips when wet) and two towels. A leather glove gets slick when wet, causing it to slip, along with being ruined. Towel one is to do the dirty work, cleaning the club-face from wet grass and mud that will clog its grooves, robbing you of control. The second towel is to thoroughly dry off your glove and grip, allowing you to have a reasonably firm grip in wet conditions.

Get The Glove On

If you're a newcomer to the game of golf and you've been playing without a glove, do yourself a favor and get one. Yes, just one – a right-handed player wears a glove on the left hand only. This is because the entirety of your left or upper hand is on the grip. Grip is the "keyword" – without a good grip, your club will move in your hands during the swing, resulting in erratic contact. This is even more needed in warm weather, when your hands tend to perspire. Moisture will make your grip feel slippery. You'll instinctively grip the club more tightly, causing you to lose clubhead speed as well as control. What's the good of investing in a set of expensive clubs if you're not well-connected to them due to the lack of a relatively cheap golf glove? A good glove, either leather or a good synthetic material, will make your hold feel more secure so you can swing more confidently and smoothly.

Equipment

MASTER·STROKES

Grip Check

The most common problem in golf is slicing the ball. If this is your problem, believe it or not, your slice could be caused by having the wrong grip – not how you hold it, but the actual grip on your club. Something as simple as having a grip that's too thick causes a slice because it restricts your wrist from releasing through impact, not allowing your clubface to square up at impact. Here's how to check your grip diameter. Hold your club in your left hand, and look to see if the tips of your middle and third fingers lightly touch against the pad of your thumb. If not, and you notice a distinctive space, it means your grip is too thick for your hands. A simple fix, and maybe the best "golf money" you've ever spent. Get your clubs re-gripped with thinner grips or less tape wound under the grips. Having clubs that fit properly in your hands will help your hands and wrists release through impact.

"Too Thick"

MASTER·STROKES

Tacky Is Good!

A real game-killer that is often overlooked by amateur golfers is as simple as the grip on their club. They don't realize how badly worn-out grips can hurt their game. When your grips are worn, you need to hold on tighter (even unconsciously) throughout the swing. You end up losing both clubhead speed and control. You should re-grip your clubs after every season if you play and practice a lot. If you don't play that often – let's say 25 to 40 times per year – you can get away with re-gripping after two seasons. A nice "tacky" grip will allow a relaxed, fluid, repetitive swing.

Lofty Expectations

Many amateurs assume equal spacing in lofts between all clubs (roughly 4 degrees apart). This is usually not true of the wedges. Most of today's pitching wedges have less loft than in the past, perhaps 44 to 46 degrees of loft. Meanwhile, most sand wedges have 56 degrees. So you may have a difference of up to 12 degrees of loft between these two clubs, way too large a "gap."

Check the loft of your wedges. If the gap is 8 degrees or more, either have the lofts bent slightly to reduce the gap, or add a "mid" or "gap" wedge with a loft midway between your sand wedge and pitching wedge. Wedge lofts that are 4 degrees apart will simplify your short-game shot choices, providing you with predictable accuracy.

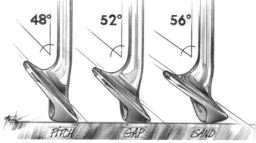

Check Your Bounce

When shopping for new wedges, remember to carefully check the bounce angle (the angle between the leading edge and the sole contact point, lowest point of the sole). Generally speaking, more bounce is better than less. More bounce greatly decreases your chances of sticking the clubhead into the ground and helps to glide the club off the turf. Let the club's bounce and face angle get the ball up in the air. Don't scoop.

bounce

Equipment

Lob Wedge Advice

Anyone over a 10 handicap will most likely not be better off with a 60-degree wedge. Most higher-handicap golfers will either have low swing speed or a poor swing plane. Either item will make high loft wedge shots super difficult. You need speed, strength and a solid golf swing to excel with the lob wedge. Drop back to a 56-degree or 57-degree sand wedge with 12 degrees, or more, of bounce. You'll do much better around the greens.

56°
yes

12°
BOUNCE

60°
Lob

Sand Wedge Wise

"A sand wedge is a sand wedge" – not true. There are a lot of differences in sand wedge designs and their performances. In particular, you need to be aware of how the sole or flange affects your shots, both out of sand traps and off grass. A wedge with a wide flange has a lot of bounce, meaning the rear of the flange is much lower than the leading edge, causing the clubhead to skid or bounce through the sand rather than dig in deep. That is why it's the right choice for green-side bunkers with soft, deep sand. On courses where the sand is firmer and there are not as many bunkers, you will be hitting more short shots off turf, so you should choose a wedge with less bounce.

It will be easier to hit these shots cleanly. Know your course and conditions, and choose the right wedge for the shots you will play most often.

Make Sure Your Putter Measures Up

Golfers experiment with their putters more than any other piece of equipment. They're hoping to find that magical putter that will drop putts.

Most concern themselves with factors such as head shape, weight or the feel at impact. Consider also whether the club's length is right for you. Most men's putters are 34, 35 or 36 inches; women's models usually range 1 inch shorter. The most common mistake is to select a putter that is too long. This will cause you to feel cramped at address and during the stroke, because your hands and forearms are hunched or backed up, rather than hanging freely. Experiment with a putter that is 1 inch shorter, and you might be surprised by the improved comfort at address and during the stroke, which can help you drop your putts.

Is Your Putter Lying?

Many amateurs have the wrong putter in their hands. They don't realize that their putter's lie is not flat to the surface when they're in their normal stroking position. They are not properly fitted to their putting stance. The most common problem is that the putter is too upright (meaning the heel is down and the toe is in the air). This can cause three problems.

First, you may catch the putter during the take-away, disrupting stroke rhythm and clubface angle. Second, you may scuff the ground through impact, slowing the face and closing it so you miss left. Third is the little-known fact that when the club rests on the heel, the slight loft makes the putterface aim slightly left of where you think you're aiming. So when you select a putter, get fitted, making sure the sole rests flat at address. You'll sink more putts.

PUTTER
ON
HEEL

Blame Game

Even the pros fall into putting slumps from time to time. They work at their mechanics and find their way out. Seniors and amateurs are more likely to blame their equipment and change putters frequently in the search for the "magic" putter. This doesn't mean you should never try another putter for a few rounds. This may give you a temporary boost in confidence.

But don't use different putters as a crutch and become a "head case."

Remember, you had success or good luck with your old putter, so there's certainly nothing wrong with it. Look more at your setup and stroke mechanics on the practice green.

This is where you'll find the problem. Once you fix it, you'll find that your good ol' putter still has the ability to sink plenty of putts for you.

Puttering Around

If you're simply enjoying your golf game, things are good. Even if you're not that competitive, you still enjoy the game more when you shoot a good score. Here's a good idea to help you do just that. Take a long iron out of your bag and start carrying two putters – a light putter to use on fast greens and a heavier putter to use on slow greens. When the greens are speedy, the light putter will enable a player to fully stroke the ball, rather than feel as though he has to baby the putt. Conversely, a heavier putter will assist the senior player on slow greens because the putter's mass will roll the ball a longer distance and not make the player feel as though he must muscle the stroke. Let the two different putters do the work, and keep your normal smooth stroke.

MASTER·STROKES

HOT Tip

Distance, distance, distance – that's what everybody seems to be focused on. Knowing this, golf-ball manufacturers heavily promote and promise that their new "HOT" ball will deliver this added distance. This is very attractive to amateurs and especially seniors who have lost distance. Beware, this extra distance comes at a price, and we don't mean $$$.

The hotter the ball is off the tee, the hotter that ball will be around the green. Longer-carrying balls don't come off the clubface with as much backspin. The ball will land at a lower angle and, with less backspin, will roll farther than you normally are used to. So, if you decide to hit a new distance ball, you need to practice your short game with it to learn how much farther your pitches, chips and sand shots will tend to roll after landing.

Hot BALL! ← HIGH SPIN BALL

Mistaken Identity

SURPRISE! You hit the wrong ball. You weren't paying attention. You walked up to where you thought you hit your drive, saw something white and round lying there, and you hit it. Not until you're lining up your ball on the green do you realize that it's not your ball.

It's a shame, too – you were having a nice hole. The penalty for this oversight is loss of hole if you're playing a match or two strokes in regular play.

From now on, make it a practice to take note of the brand and type of ball you are playing, and put an identifying mark on your ball. Like the pros, you need your mark because someone in your group could be playing the same model. Also, on busy courses, you come across lost balls you might mistake for your own. Wake up.

Be A Good Scout – Be Prepared!

Did you ever play a round of golf with someone who rushed to the first tee, only to constantly search during the rest of the round for things he needed to play?

Annoying, right? It's good etiquette to have everything you need, where and when you need it. Not being prepared is inconsiderate, because it is disruptive to your playing partners. It's also detrimental to your own game. Here is a good habit for golfers to get into. Before you get to the first tee, put nongolf items (keys, wallet, cell phone – OFF!) in a separate pocket or golf-bag compartment. Then have one pocket where you keep the following: eight to 10 golf tees, a small coin or ball marker, a green repair tool to fix ball marks and clean your spikes, and an extra ball in case you need a provisional. Finally, always have a small towel attached to your golf bag. Being organized helps speed play, leading to a good flow or rhythm to the game that benefits all.

YAK YAK YAK

SECTION 3:
Rules & Etiquette

More than perhaps any other game, golf frowns upon players who fail to follow its rules or adhere to its code of etiquette. Those rules and that code can sometimes seem complicated, even counterintuitive. The tips in this chapter will help you deftly navigate some of the most common and confusing golf ethics and etiquette scenarios.

CONTENTS

MASTER·STROKES

Juggling Balls

It's pretty common to see amateur golfers using different golf balls during their round. The logic is to use certain types of golf balls for different types of shots (for example, a low-flying ball for shots into a strong wind). If you're playing a casual game of golf with buddies, this is OK. During some competitions, a local rule will require that you play the same USGA-approved brand and model ball throughout the round. You're allowed to use more than one ball during such rounds, but if you do switch, your new ball must be the identical brand and model you started your round with. Check the local "one ball" rules before a competition. Decide what ball design will be best for a given course and weather conditions, and put several in your bag before teeing off.

Section 3:

Freeze, Partner!

Have you ever been in a foursome in which one of your group who has already teed off starts walking down the fairway as you're about to hit? Unbelievably, there are golfers who actually do this. Now, if your first thought is—that this is terrible etiquette, of course you're right, but keep in mind that this is also dangerous. It's very possible that these walkers could be "taken out" with a wayward shot. On the proper-etiquette side, this rude behavior is very distracting to other players when they are attempting their shot. If you are in the fairway waiting for a player behind you to hit, be sure to keep your eyes on the player as he or she swings, or you'll never know what might be coming your way.

Rules & Etiquette

Changing Club's Makeup During Play

Are you allowed to change the playing characteristics of your club during a round? Some golfers add lead tape to their clubhead to simply add weight or, by placing it toward either the heel or the toe, to alter its center of gravity. Let's say you have a driver you have added tape to, and you have been hitting it well. But you decide, after several holes of a round in your club championship, that it feels too heavy. So you remove the lead strips to lighten it up for the remainder of the round. You use the driver on the next hole. Is this a legal move? Absolutely not. Removing the lead tape constitutes a change in playing characteristics of the club during the round, and the penalty for this is disqualification.

Damage Control

You're playing a competitive round, you reach for your "trusty" old putter, and as you pull it out of the bag, it gets caught, causing you to drop it. It hits the concrete cart path, and surprisingly, the head snaps off. What do the rules allow you to do?

If any club is accidentally damaged during play, the rules state that you may replace it with another club, although the replacement may not be a club being used by another player on the course. Also, any replacement must be made without unduly delaying play. Note: If you deliberately damage or break a club during play (throwing a tantrum?), you may not replace it during the round.

Rules & Etiquette

Coming Through

Your opponent just hit a sweet drive right down the middle. You step up to the plate and answer right back. You're just as sweet, and when your ball finally comes to a rest, it's actually just a few inches behind his. They almost touched, but you're away. When you get up to your ball, they're so close that you ask him to lift his ball, fearing your ball might hit his as yours takes off.

He claims that under the rules he's not allowed. Who's right?

You are. If the opponent's ball in any way impedes your swing or stance, the opponent must lift the ball if requested, then replace it at the marked spot. In stroke play, the golfer whose ball is impeding the other ball may opt to play his ball first, rather than lift it.

Landscaping 101

You just hit a great tee shot down the middle of the fairway. You can't wait to get to your ball, but when you do you find it is sitting in a divot hole. This is one of the most frustrating experiences in golf. The ensuing shot is, if not impossible, very difficult. Don't be "that guy" we get mad at because he simply walks away after taking a deep divot. If playing on bentgrass fairways, the divot will usually be in one piece. Simply place it back and tamp it down. If you're playing on Bermuda fairways, where the divot tends to "spray," you should not try to replace it. Instead, kick in the edges of the divot, as this aids the regrowing process. On the tees of par-3 holes, fill the divot with the sand/fertilizer mixture, which is often available.

Rules & Etiquette

Sticky Situation

The fall winds have left more tree branches and twigs than normal along the fairway, and your tee shot has just found one. You have a clear shot to the green, but a branch is lying up against the front of your ball. It will probably affect the flight of your shot if you leave it. Can it be removed?

Yes. A branch is classified as a loose impediment. When your ball is not lying in a hazard, as is the case here, the rules allow you to remove a loose impediment from around the ball with no penalty. However, if in removing the impediment you should move the ball, you would have to add a one-stroke penalty. So before doing anything, look carefully at the position of the branch. If you think the ball will move when removing the branch, you're better off leaving the branch and playing the ball as it lies.

Silence Is Golden

"What was that beep?" "Who's texting you?" "Get off that phone!" "Quiet – I am trying to hit!"

Are you talking to your kids? Not anymore. It seems like the whole world is one constant text message, and we all have a cellphone permanently glued to our ears, seniors included. What happened to manners? Golf is a sport that thankfully holds sportsmanship and etiquette in high regard, and the golf course has always been a wonderful respite from a hectic and LOUD world. An important part of good etiquette is to stay absolutely quiet while an opponent is setting up to play and then hitting the shot. Any sudden noise or conversation can distract or unsettle a player. So be considerate and preserve a beautiful part of the game by respectfully turning off all your gadgets, and refrain from talking at the wrong time. There's plenty of time to converse while you are walking a fairway or waiting for a foursome ahead to putt out.

MASTER·STROKES

Get Relief!

You're playing a match and you hit a shot that runs off the side of the fairway and comes to rest on a cart path. You need to take a drop at the nearest point of relief within one club length of the cart path but no closer to the hole. You drop the ball, you take your stance with one heel still touching the cart path, and you hit your shot. The next thing you hear is your opponent telling you that you just lost the hole. Is that correct?

Yes. When you drop your ball away from an obstruction, you must make sure both the ball and your stance are completely free from the obstruction before hitting your next shot. The penalty would be loss of hole in match play or two strokes in stroke play.

Instructions On Immovable Obstructions

A golf course that you're playing has electrical power lines traversing it. Of course, your ball ended up at the base of one of the towers, blocking your next shot. Your opponent says you must take a one-shot penalty to move your ball away from it. Is he correct?

According to the rules, when your ball comes to a rest on or against any man-made, immovable obstruction, or the obstruction interferes with your stance or intended area of swing, you are entitled to relief without penalty. Drop the ball within one club-length of the edge of the obstruction to a spot no nearer the hole, which provides relief from the obstruction.

MASTER·STROKES

'Yo Mo, Don't Be Slow!'

It's OK to enjoy a round of golf even if you or your partners are not very good. The game is for everyone. That being said, it doesn't mean you own the course and you don't have to be considerate to the other groups of players behind you. Slow play can be a big problem. One slow group that takes five hours to play a round causes everyone behind it to also take five hours.

If one or more of your group is struggling and you've noticed the foursome behind you is constantly waiting for you to get out of range, wave them ahead and let them play through. This is proper course etiquette. It also benefits you and your group by taking the heat off. Golf isn't fun with people breathing down your neck. You'll all play better being more relaxed.

MASTER·STROKES

A lot goes into maintaining golf courses, especially in the spring after a long, hard winter. There will be times you will find that your ball ends up in an area that is undergoing improvement – commonly know as "ground under repair." These areas usually will be marked with a sign, string or lines drawn. When this happens, you may do the following without penalty: Drop the ball within one club length of the "ground under repair" area, no closer to the hole, and in a position where the area has no effect on either your stance or swing. Keep in mind that when your ball is in an area under repair and your swing is clear, you may choose to play the ball as it lies.

Rough Neighborhood

136

TARGET

MASTER·STROKES

Is Ball In Hazard Lost?

You just smoked your tee shot right down the middle of the fairway – feels good. You know this hole has a pond 270 yards out, but you normally wouldn't reach it. So, not concerned, you walk straight toward where you expect to find your ball, and there's nothing, no ball. Right ahead of you is the pond. You assume you must have hit one extra-sweet and reached the hazard. You decide to drop another ball behind the approximate point of entry. Slightly annoyed, you plan on taking a one-stroke penalty. Then your opponent says: "Your ball is lost. You must go back to the tee and take a stroke and distance penalty." Is he right?

No. In this case, there is reasonable evidence that the ball is in the pond. Therefore, even though you didn't find the ball, you can fairly assume the ball reached the hazard and take just the one-stroke penalty.

MASTER·STROKES

Hazardous Work

You just hit your ball short of a narrow creek. It skipped over and ended up on the top of the opposite bank. That's great! Your ball is dry, and you can hit it. As you set up, you hear your playing partner say, "Don't ground your club, the ball's in the hazard." You reply: "My ball isn't in the water. I can totally ground my club." Who's right?

The rules state that all ground or water within the area marked as a water hazard is part of the hazard. The boundaries will be marked by yellow stakes. If your ball lies inside an imaginary line drawn between the stakes (which is most likely if your ball is below the top edge of the bank), it is within the hazard. You cannot ground your club before hitting your shot.

don't ground club

65

MASTER·STROKES

High-Stakes Golf

As you look up from hitting your tee shot, you watch your ball land and roll out of the fairway, then stop alongside a water hazard. Not good, but it should be playable. When you set up to play your recovery shot, you notice that your backswing is impeded by a stake marking the hazard. You pull out the stake, take your next shot and then replace the stake. "You just lost the hole," says your opponent. Is this correct?

No. You were within the rules. A hazard stake (unlike an out-of-bounds stake) is considered a movable obstruction. You may remove it to play the shot, whether your ball is within or outside the hazard, with no penalty.

Rough Relief?

Your approach shot landed a few feet off the green in the rough and came to rest on a sprinkler head. You say you're entitled to a free drop within one club length of the nearest point of relief, no closer to the hole. Your opponent agrees. You move to this point of relief and find that this would allow you to drop your ball on the close-cut apron of the green, which would then allow you to putt the ball. Your opponent is upset and claims you must drop your ball in the rough. Is this correct?

No. The rules do not differentiate between "rough" and the fairway or the green's apron. All these areas are simply considered "through the green." As long as you drop at the spot that provides the nearest relief from the obstruction for your stance and swing, the ball can be dropped on close-cut grass rather than in the rough.

67   **Rules & Etiquette**

Do You Take A Drop Correctly?

When you are taking a drop during the course of play, either a free drop or one in which you are incurring a penalty, you must drop the ball by the rules. The rule book prescribes that to drop correctly at the determined spot, stand erect with your arm extended fully at shoulder height, and drop the ball so that it lands without touching you. If you fail to drop correctly, you may lift and drop the ball again without penalty. However, if you fail to make the drop in the correct manner and go on to play your shot, the penalty is one stroke.

You Got Plugged

The golf course is very soft and wet after a long winter and a rainy spring. Your high approach shot is short and a little off line. It lands on the upslope of a green-side bank – you don't see it bounce. As you get to your ball, you find it seriously "plugged." You tell your opponent you want to take a free drop. He answers: "Not happening. You must play your ball as it lies because it landed in rough rather than a closely mown area." Who's right?

This one is tricky! According to the rules, an embedded ball may be lifted, cleaned and dropped only if it lies in a "closely mown" area (mown to fairway height or less). However, local rules will usually allow you to lift, clean and drop (no nearer to the hole) when the ball is embedded anywhere on the course when wet conditions prevail. Moral:

Learn the club's local rules before you tee off.

MASTER·STROKES

Cleaning Up A Muddy Situation

This spring, you will be looking down on quite a few balls with mud on them. What's the rule about cleaning them off?

Rule 21: The ball must not be cleaned, unless it lies on the putting green. The ball is considered on the green if any part of it is touching the green.

If your ball is on the fringe surrounding the green or putting surface, you may not lift and clean it. A ball on the putting green may be cleaned when lifted under rule 16-b.

Elsewhere, a ball may be cleaned when lifted, except when it has been lifted:

A) to determine if it's unfit for play;

B) for identification, in which case it may be cleaned only to the extent necessary for identification; or

C) because it is assisting or interfering with play.

If a player cleans his ball during play of a hole except as provided in this rule, he incurs a penalty of one stroke, and the ball, if lifted, must be replaced.

MASTER·STROKES

Double Dip

You're in really nasty, weedy, deep rough. Your clubhead comes down very "fat," weakly popping the ball up just a few inches into the air and allowing your clubhead to hit the ball a second time during the same stroke. Your ball deflects off into the same garbage.

This problem usually occurs on short shots, where the speed of the clubhead is slow to begin with, plus the clubhead is snuffed completely by the heavy rough. Is there any penalty? If this happens, you must count a total of two strokes, one for each time the clubhead contacted the ball. You now have to play your ball from where it rests.

Rules & Etiquette

It's Nuts Out There

It's a beautiful fall day, and you've seen more squirrels than normal during your round. You hit a pitch-and-roll shot from off the green, and it's heading for the cup when a squirrel suddenly zips across the green and collides with your ball, deflecting it way off to the side, far from the hole. You insist that you can replay the shot, but your opponent says that's not happening. Who's correct?

Your opponent is. When a ball hit from off the green is deflected by any "outside agency" (which includes animals), the stroke counts, and the ball must be played from where it came to rest. Keep in mind, however, that if you were to hit a putt from on the green that was deflected by any outside agency, you would be allowed to replay the stroke without penalty.

Get To The Bottom Of It

You just "holed" an awesome long approach shot, or a pitch or a chip that ended up in the cup.

Or you think you did. Before you start celebrating that you holed out, you notice that you can still see your ball because it is pinned between the flagstick and the edge of the cup. It's in, but it didn't drop. What's the ruling?

Be careful, because if you go up to the flag and yank it out and the ball comes out with it, it doesn't count. The rules state that if this occurs, you have to place the ball on the lip, then tap it in, losing a stroke. So make sure in a situation like this that you move the flagstick away carefully so your ball has room to fall in and you get your reward.

Rules & Etiquette

Squishy Situation

It's been raining a lot, so you're not surprised when you get out onto the course that it's wet in places, but you can play. You hit your tee shot and, after walking up to your ball, you find that it's lying in a soggy area. How do you know if you are entitled to drop the ball away from what you think is "casual water"? According to the rules, casual water is any water not within a water hazard and that is visible around the ball either before or after you take your stance. If you're not sure there is casual water, assume your stance. If you can see water rising up around the soles of your shoes, you may drop the ball within one club length of the nearest point of relief, no nearer to the hole. Final note: You may only claim casual water if your natural stance raises water, as opposed to pressing down extra-hard with your feet.

WATER →

Spring Showers

In the spring, we normally get plenty of rain, so it's not unusual to find water around the course and puddles on the green. What can you do about it?

Let's clear up the rules. If your ball is resting in casual water on the green (or anywhere else), you are allowed to move it. You must determine the nearest point of relief – no closer to the hole. You may then place the ball within one club length of this point at which the casual water ends. This rule does not mean you can choose to place the ball on either side of the casual-water area. You must place the ball at the point of nearest relief from the original spot.

X
PLACE BALL

Rules & Etiquette

Double Trouble?

Your approach shot goes in the hole. No, not that hole – the hole burrowed by some critter in the green-side bunker you just landed in. This burrowed hole, probably done by a rabbit, mole or gopher, also is up against the lip. This would be a "nightmare" of a shot.

The question is, is this situation considered an obstruction that would hopefully grant you relief?

You say you're allowed a free drop. Your opponent says no. He claims you can't move your ball because it's in a hazard. Who's right?

You are. Under the rules, if the ball finds a burrow hole within a bunker, you may drop the ball at the nearest point of relief, no closer to the hole and still within the bunker, with no penalty.

Don't Get RAKED OVER

Most of us hate raking, but we all appreciate why rakes are lying in sand traps. Let's say you just found your ball lying against one of these rakes after you hit into a green-side bunker. You carefully reach into the sand trap to lift the rake away, but as you do, your ball moves slightly. Your opponent aggressively says, "Your ball moved, that's a one-stroke penalty." Is it? NO! In the rules, it states that an object such as a rake is a movable obstruction, from which the player is allowed relief. If in removing the obstruction the ball also moves, it must be replaced into its original position. There is no penalty.

MASTER·STROKES

Beach And High Tide

You just resumed play after a rainstorm, and you hit your shot into a green-side bunker. You find the ball sitting in a large puddle.

Can you get relief? Yes, if your ball is in casual water (temporary accumulation of water) in a bunker, the ball may be dropped at the nearest spot to where the ball lies no nearer the hole, in a part of the bunker that offers the maximum available relief. For instance, if the entire bunker is covered with water, the player may drop the ball in the shallowest part of the bunker no nearer the hole. NOTE: Under penalty of one stroke, the player may drop a ball on a line between where the ball lies and the hole, but no nearer to the hole. You do have the option of playing the ball from where it originally rested in the bunker.

Play Nice In The Sand

Many amateurs and seniors who are new to the game are not aware of all the rules. Do you know this sand rule? Let's say you address your ball in a greenside bunker with the sole of your sand wedge correctly hovering slightly above the sand. As you start back, the sole clips a raised bit of sand a few inches behind the ball. After you complete the shot, your opponent says you must take a penalty for grounding your club in a hazard. You argue that it's OK to touch the hazard once the swing has begun. Who's correct?

Your opponent is. When the ball is resting in a hazard, the club must not touch the hazard at any time prior to impact. Penalty is loss of hole in match play, two strokes in stroke play.

Rules & Etiquette

Combo?

You're just off the green with a nice, smooth lie, so you decide to putt your ball to the flag. Because of the break, you need to aim right (where your opponent's ball lies, on the green) to allow your ball to break left. Your ball accidentally hits your opponent's ball, deflecting it farther right while your ball goes left, closer to the hole. Are you in trouble?

No. According to the rules, if a player's ball in motion after a stroke is deflected or stopped by a ball in play and at rest, the player must play his ball as it lies. In match play, there is no penalty. In stroke play, there is no penalty unless both balls lie on the putting green prior to the stroke, in which case the player incurs a penalty of two strokes. As far as the other ball is concerned, if a player's ball is moved by another ball in motion caused by a stroke, the moved ball must be replaced without penalty to the player. Because you were hitting from off the green, there is no penalty. Play from where your ball came to rest and replace your opponent's ball to the best of your ability.

Polite Par-3

You will notice on busy courses that long par-3s will get the most backed up. This is because the majority of amateurs miss the green. This leads to them needing to play two, three or four more shots to hole out, while foursomes wait behind them. If this is the case with your group, make it a practice to let others play through. When you're on the green of a long par-3 and you notice foursomes waiting behind you, wave to the next foursome to hit their tee shots. Stand far enough away so no one gets hit. Then your group can return to the green and putt out as the next group is walking up. This etiquette will help keep a nice, steady pace on the course. It also gets pressure off your backs and helps make your outing more enjoyable.

Rules & Etiquette

More Damage Control

You just hit a nice approach shot, landing your ball just a couple of feet away from the hole. Birdie time! Or not? You walk up to find that the side of the hole your ball needs to go over is damaged in such a way that it even appears dented in. This could easily get in the way of you sinking your putt. You attempt to fix the hole by pushing back on the inside to get the hole back to a perfect circle. Is there anything wrong with this?

Yes. According to the rules, you may not repair any damage to the putting green (of which the hole is a part) if such repair might assist your play of the hole. The penalty for this is two strokes in stroke play and loss of the hole in match play. **Note:** You may repair the hole once play of the hole is completed.

Landscaping?

Even with the changeover to "soft" spikes from the old metal spikes, golfers still come across spike marks in their line of putt. Of course, this can really cost you. Can you tap down and repair these marks to help you sink that all-important putt? Unfortunately, the answer is NO! The rule states that, unlike with ball marks that you may repair, marks made by spiked golf shoes along your line may not be tapped down. The penalty for breaking this rule is two strokes in stroke play and loss of hole in match play. After the hole is completed, it is allowed, along with being good etiquette to clean up any spike marks before leaving the green.

Polite Putting

It's probably happened to you – you're about to hit a very important putt when you catch someone, out of the corner of your eye, move or just standing where you can see him. This distraction breaks your concentration and lessens your odds for success. All golfers are different, but most want to focus only on the ball and hole while putting. So be considerate and make sure you are standing well away from the person who is putting. Never be in his putting line, either behind or in front. Stand at a quartering angle to his line of putt. Adopt this good etiquette, "out of sight, out of mind."

MASTER·STROKES

HELP?

Golf is one of those games that you're on your own. The number on your score card is the result of what you did, no one else. A slight exception is that you may receive advice from a playing partner or caddie before you putt. According to the rules, they are allowed to help point out or suggest a line of roll or where they think a putt will break as long as they don't physically touch the green.

NO!

Once you are over the ball – that is, in the act of putting – no one can continue to help. They can't mark or even point to a spot that they think is the expected line or aim point in any way. It's all you. The penalty for breaking this rule is two strokes in stroke play, and loss of hole in match play.

Rules & Etiquette

MASTER·STROKES

Moving Day

It's a very windy fall day, with a lot of leaves blowing around. You're away, so you mark your ball on the green with a coin. Now it's your turn. You pick up the coin and replace your ball. After reading your putt but before you take your stance, you see that the ball has moved from its original position. Do you take a penalty stroke?

In this case, the answer is no. You have not caused the ball to move by making contact with it, nor did you have your feet in position to play the stroke with your clubhead "grounded" behind the ball when it moved. You may play your next shot with no penalty from where the ball now rests.

Bumper Ball?

You're playing a match and you hit your putt, leaving your ball just one inch outside the cup. Your ball happens to be to the right of your opponent's putting line. You walk up to tap it in when you hear your opponent say, "Leave it there!" If his or her putt misses to the right, it might deflect off your ball back to the left and into the hole. Do you have to leave your ball as asked? No. The rules state that any putter may lift his or her ball if he or she decides that the ball's position might help the opposing player.

MASTER·STROKES

'Harry, Keep The Change'

As your playing partner lines up his putt, he asks you to mark your ball, which is closer to the hole and arguably in his line.

You don't have a ball marker, so you reach into your pocket and realize you're flat out of change.

To solve the problem, you take a tee and place it in the ground just behind your ball to mark its position. You tell your partner, "Sorry, pal, that will have to do, I don't have a dime."

He doesn't think you're funny and exclaims, "That's not legal!" Is he right?

Yes, he is. The rules call for a ball lying on the green to be marked with a small coin or similar flat object. A tee sticking out of the ground would still deflect the other player's putt, should the ball strike it. Next time, be better prepared by making sure you have everything you need, including a ball marker or some spare change.

Section 3:

Don't Gimme No Lip

Remember Tiger Woods' ball balancing on the very lip of the cup after chipping at the 16th hole at Augusta during the 2005 Masters? It felt like an eternity. We watched his ball eventually drop to help him go on to win that championship. How long did he wait?

Let's say you just hit an amazing putt or chip, and your ball is hanging. How long can you wait? What's the rule?

According to the rules, once you've hit your putt, you're expected to walk to the hole without any undue delay. When you've reached your ball and the hole, you may wait a maximum of 10 seconds to see if the ball will drop in. If you delay any longer than that, under the rules, you must take a one-stroke penalty. You're on the clock – tick, tick, tick.

MASTER·STROKES

Practice Is Cheating?

When the bell rings and your round of golf has started, PRACTICE IS OVER! You are not permitted to play any practice shots either during the play of the hole or between holes.

There is one exception: You may practice putting or chipping either on or near the green of the hole just completed, on the next tee or on any nearby practice putting green (not another green on the course itself). Of course, use good etiquette.

If convicted, your penalty is two strokes in stroke play, or loss of the next hole to be played in match play.

Etiquette For Idiots

The weather is great, and everyone came out to play a round. Of course, that can cause a backup on holes. So why is some guy in the group ahead of you practicing his putting after everyone in his foursome holed out? Because he is rude! Just because he missed his "real" putt doesn't give him the right to try it again in order to learn something or build a little confidence. This is very poor etiquette when a group behind is waiting to play to the green. Remember, if you really need to hit a practice putt, do so only after checking to see that no one in the group behind you is ready to play to the green. Good etiquette helps everyone enjoy the game.

Rules & Etiquette

MASTER·STROKES

You're On The Clock

You're a recreational golfer who doesn't play that much, so you might not know all the rules. You're playing in a golf outing, and you hit your tee shot into the woods. You have a good idea where it went into the trees. When you get to where you think your ball should be, you don't see a ball. How long do you have to look for it before you must decide it is lost and take a penalty? According to the rules, you have five minutes from the moment you (or your partner or your caddie) reach the area where you think your ball has stopped. If you don't find it within that period, you must go back to the tee and play another ball, at a penalty of one stroke plus distance.

MASTER·STROKES

Read It Or Weep!

Your opponent has accidentally made a mistake on your scorecard. After the round, you don't pick up the mistake, and you go ahead and sign it. Who's at fault, and what happens?

The answer is, you are at fault, and you will be disqualified if the score you signed for is actually lower than you shot. If the score you signed for is higher than you shot, you must accept the higher score as marked. The best way to avoid this is to check each hole as you play, then double-check the math before signing the scorecard and turning it in.

Rules & Etiquette

What's Your Handicap?

Many casual recreational golfers do not know their established handicap. Here's how to compute one:

1. Record scores for 20 rounds, along with the course rating of the tees played from.

2. Subtract course rating from score (for example, 92-70.5 = 21.5).

3. Take the 10 best scores (lowest amounts above the course ratings). Add those numbers and divide by 10. Then multiply this number by 96 percent.

Example: Your 10 best of 20 scores total 177 strokes above the course ratings. Divide by 10; you average 17.7 strokes above the course rating per round. Multiply 17.7 by 96 percent; your current handicap is 17.0. Add future rounds and delete the oldest scores to keep your handicap current.

SECTION 4:
Practice Drills

Practice may not make you perfect; there's no such thing as perfect in golf. But practice can make you a lot better, and, in the process, a lot more satisfied on the golf course. These drills will help you master the basics and nuances of golf's short game.

CONTENTS

Location, Location, Location!

We have all heard the three most important rules of the real estate game. Well, the three most important rules of the golf game are "practice, practice, practice!" If you never take a lesson or if you don't even know the right equipment to use, you'll still improve if you practice. The area that you will benefit the most from practicing is the "short game." If you have a high handicap, it is probably finding you off the green after your tee shot and long iron. Being off the green makes it even more essential to have a tidy short game. You need to make the decision to commit the majority of your practice time to your short game – pitches from 50 yards and closer, chipping, sand shots and putting – as opposed to always hitting full shots at the driving range. Stick with this practice philosophy for the entire season, and you'll find yourself with the best score your game will allow.

Practice Drills

MASTER·STROKES

Are Drills Really Important?

The Drill Sergeant thinks so, YES SIR! Athletes in all sports work on drills to perfect their body actions and tune their muscles. Golf has lagged far behind other sports in this regard. To get better faster, by all means use appropriate drills. They will speed your improvement. So design your own "boot camp" and be battle-ready.

Bank Job

Offseason practice is like "money in the bank." Too many amateur golfers completely shut it down during the winter, and then they wonder why their game never gets any better year after year. They start the new season off rusty and out of shape. It takes a while just to get back to where you were the season before. What they need to do is continue advancing their game and maintain the fundamentals throughout the winter doldrums. There are many ways to commit to this goal. Exercise, drills, heated driving ranges, golf getaways and indoor practice all will help keep your game reasonably sharp. An offseason workout/practice regimen will help you come out of the gate ready to make next season a breakout year with a big advance in your game. The offseason doesn't have to be wasted time and potentially a regression of your abilities.

MASTER·STROKES

Practice Versus Play

Practice is for improvement. Play is for enjoyment. Enjoyment is shooting your best score.

Many amateurs make the mistake of trying to "find their game" on the golf course during play. This is not the time or place to experiment trying to solve a swing problem. The practice tee is where you fix faults and reinforce sound fundamentals so you can repeat them during play under pressure. If you've identified a problem in your swing and are sure of the adjustment needed, implement the fix at practice. Practice is when you try for perfection in your mechanics, not worrying if the adjustment feels strange and you hit some bad shots at first. When you're playing, try to win or shoot your best score – don't worry about your swing. With time, the motions you're working on at the practice tee will show up more and more when you're out on the course.

Practice Game Plan

When you head out to the practice range, you should have a plan in mind to help improve your game. That sounds obvious, but believe me, most amateurs don't do this. They typically grab a bucket of balls and hit a few shots with every club. Another common mistake you see all the time is that amateurs spend most of their practice hitting their driver. That doesn't help give you the complete game you need out on the course. Your practice will benefit you the most if you identify the weakest part of your game, whether it is driving, iron play, short game or putting. Focus the majority of your practice on this weakness. Over time, you will see a marked improvement in what used to be the worst part of your game. It might be more fun to hit your "favorite" clubs, but by working hard on your weakness, you'll start posting some "favorite" scores.

Practice Drills

Good Start

You have just finished the first few holes of your round of golf and you're already FINISHED! Your round is already shot because you got off to such a terrible start. You can keep this from happening if you would only commit – and we mean religiously – to a brief warm-up session before EVERY round. This is critical for seniors, who tend to be less flexible than younger players.

The goal of the warm-up is not to perfect your swing; it is simply to loosen up the old muscles and joints, and to get the feel of the ball and observe any particular flight pattern to your shots. Just hitting 15 balls – three balls with every third club – will give you an indicator of what to expect. This will give you a chance to make early adjustments and help you get off to a good start.

Slow-Motion Practice

Amateur golfers go to the driving range in the worthy pursuit of improving their game. What happens too often is that they hit a ton of balls at a very fast pace in a very short time. They think this must be good – it's practice, right? Wrong. It's not good, and it's not practice. Practice is supposed to improve your game. The end result isn't swing improvement, it's swing damage. The excessive amount of swings and the fast pace cause amateurs to speed up their swing tempo and lose track of swing fundamentals.

A better approach is to try to practice in slow motion. Make each swing count. Take your time between shots. Think about your pre-shot routine. Set up to the ball meticulously. Each swing should have a purpose. Try to keep your swing tempo extra slow. Observe the ball's flight, and think about what was positive or negative about the swing you just made. Put it in your file and learn from it. You'll have more productive practices, and your shot making will be improved when you get back out on the course.

Practice Drills

Get REAL!

We often hear complaints from amateurs and seniors that they don't understand why they struggle so much out on the course but hit the ball well at the practice range. Well, the golf course is not the practice range. Out on the course fairway, you will have rolling, hilly terrain, leaving you with many unlevel shots. The practice range is flat, so you're always hitting from level stances. In the real world, you'll be facing shots with the ball above or below your feet, or the lie is uphill or downhill.

To be ready to take on the real world, you must make it a point to practice from these types of lies. Search around for a range that has a practice tee with sloping sides. This will allow you to practice hitting balls above or below your feet. If you find a raised teeing area, you can work on hitting from uphill and downhill lies.

Section 4: 106

Give Your Joints Some 'R&R' Rather Than 'ER'

Unfortunately, many casual golfers gradually develop pain in their joints while making their swing.

The pain most often occurs in their hands, wrists, elbows and shoulders. If this is you, it could get to the point where you are playing less and almost never practicing. Of course, you will see a deterioration in your game. Here's an idea that will help. When you do get back to practicing, start using a tee with all your clubs. That's right, a tee – with your irons, too. You only need to tee the ball up a quarter of an inch. Don't hit the dirt! Think of all the swings you hit with a bucket or two. Using a tee will avoid a tremendous amount of stress that radiates up your hands and arms every time your clubhead smashes into the turf. You'll have less pain and injury over the long run. Your joints will thank you.

MASTER·STROKES

Playing In Bad Weather

Tom Watson was considered the best
poor-weather player in the history of the
game. Here's why:

   1) He was always prepared. He had
rain gear, waterproof shoes, extra socks, gloves,
hand warmers and a rain suit.

   2) Tom always played in bad weather. When it
was cold and rainy outside, he went out and
practiced in it.

   3) Watson ignored the bad conditions once
he was in them. He knew the other players
were facing the same weather, too.

   In poor weather, everyone is in the same
boat. If you're prepared, you can be the one
to ignore the conditions and focus on
your shots.

Left Thumb, Right

It's critical that you have strong club support with your left hand through impact. This is especially important for seniors, who have possibly lost some hand strength. Without good left-hand support, your clubhead will slow down right before impact, causing a "DEAD" feel through impact and resulting in a loss of power and distance. To guard against this, it's important that your left hand be positioned correctly on your grip to help withstand the force of impact. Make sure that when you close your left hand around the club, the middle of your left thumb is well to the right of the top-center of the shaft, rather than right on top or left.

A good drill to test this is hitting one-handed chip shots with your left thumb placed on the right side of the grip. Then hit some with your thumb centered on top of the grip. You will feel a big difference at impact, convincing you that you'll get a much more solid feel and more speed with your left thumb correctly placed on the right side of the grip.

Swing Under

A common error that can strike casual golfers is swinging over the top. They tend to stand up too straight at address, lacking spine tilt away from the target. This simply means that the shoulders are swinging level during the downswing. This throws the arms out of plane across the body, usually resulting in a slice. A great drill is to take a club and place the left hand on top of the club with the head on the ground and swing the right arm to the top and then down under the left forearm. This will give you the correct feel of how the shoulders work. The right side will be lower, which places the club on an inside-out swing path. This is a great drill for those who slice the ball.

MASTER·STROKES

Pump It Up

The pump drill is one of the best ways to get the club on an inside-out path. Take your normal setup and swing the club back halfway. The picture represents the pumping action of three times up and back down, making sure each time you bring the club down that the shaft stays in line with the right forearm and the wrist angle is still cocked. On the third pump, you swing down and try to feel the previous two rehearsal pumps, and the club will follow the muscle memory of this. This is a great drill for slicers.

Practice Drills

Extend The Triangle

A common error in the golf swing is a
lack of extension during the takeaway. This is
especially true for golfers who have lost a
little flexibility and strength, causing
erratic swings. In this drill you will see
the club handle positioned in the
belt buckle and my arms
extended down the
shaft. Simply turn
back but keep the
club attached to the belt,
not allowing it to come off. You will see the
right forearm is higher than the left, which is
a perfect position for swinging the club
upward into the backswing. This gives the
arms, hands and shoulders that "one piece" or
"triangular" takeaway. This is vital to get back
that repeatable swing.

SHOULDERS
ARMS
HANDS
TRIANGLE

ONE-PIECE TAKEAWAY

BELT
BUCKLE

MASTER·STROKES

Push The Board

If you are working on a one-piece takeaway and can't seem to get the feel, this drill is for you. The drill promotes a good shoulder turn mainly because you must use the large muscles of the shoulders to move the board back. Place the board on your intended target line with just enough room to place your club between the board and ball. As you start to push the board back, you will feel the shoulders winding up as the board moves completely out of the way of the swing. The key is to push the board back and continue through to the completion of the swing.

113   Practice Drills

Full Shoulder Turn

I like to use visual aids to
help with feel. In the picture you will see a Sharpie
pen. This is used so that I
can feel the shoulder
turning using the pen as a
reference. Many times the
shoulder or head dips down
instead of staying level during
the swing. The rotation should
feel like the shoulder is turning
more under the pen while holding
the head steady. If you lift the shoulders, you will knock the pen out, and if
you tilt the shoulders, you will see that the
shoulders have not made a turn at all. This
gives you the proper feedback to make a better turn.

Level Wings SLICE!

Open shoulders is one common cause of slicing the ball. Most amateur golfers suffer this problem, and they don't know why. They believe their shoulders are square to the target line if they get them nice and level at address. Actually, your tour pro's spine tilts away from the target about 10 degrees. A drill to help correct this is called the "Airplane Drill." This is because you put your arms out straight, then bank them to the right as if you're turning an airplane. Stand upright with no club, and spread your arms out to form a "T." Then tilt your spine just a bit, so that the tip of your left hand rises by about 8-10 inches, and the right hand lowers by the same amount. Notice that with your arms out you can feel proper spine tilt very clearly. Next, drop your arms down into a relaxed address position. Remember this feeling. To help ingrain this correct tilt into your address for straight shots to replace that slice, you need to make this drill part of your regular exercise.

One-Arm Swinger

A great way to develop tempo along with a good pivot is to try this "One-Arm Drill." Grip the club using your right-hand grip (left hand for lefties) and make a few waist-high to waist-high swings. You want to make sure that you control the clubhead by making a good pivot with the shoulders while also making your wrist set. If you cannot hit this shot, the primary reason is the hand is slapping at the ball, which is usually caused by a quick swinging motion that lacks a good pivot. Remember, swing slow, control the club and be firm through the impact area as you turn through to the finish.

Stand Firm

If you are having trouble with hips that are sliding or tilting, this is the drill for you. Place an umbrella in the ground by the back of your right heel. As you are swinging back, your key is not to push against the umbrella or knock it over. The umbrella should stay firmly in the ground while the lower body remains stable. Excessive movement, especially in the lower body, will result in off-balance shots and a very inconsistent ball flight pattern. The key to a repeatable swing is a stable lower body, so give this drill a try for a cure for an overactive lower body.

Practice Drills

Good Credit Score

Many golfers tend to overswing on the backswing and take the club way past parallel at the top of the swing. Overswinging will always result in erratic shots. We have found this simple tip really assists our students in tightening up and shortening the backswing. Put a credit card under the left armpit (for right-handers) between the upper left arm and left breast. Now go ahead and make swings, being certain not to drop the credit card out from under the armpit on your backswing. Immediately you will have a shorter and crisper backswing, which will lead to better ball striking with more accurate shots.

SHORTEN BACKSWING

Claw Drill
For Better Arm Swing

A drill that's easy to do and great for feel is the claw drill. Take your right hand and clasp under your left wrist. Now swing the club to the top of your backswing. This drill forces the left arm to swing more on the proper plane. This drill is especially good if you swing your left arm too upright, which means that the left arm is closer to your head than the right shoulder. This drill also keeps the right elbow in the correct position at the top, and places the left arm more across the chest.

MASTER·STROKES

**Balancing
Act**

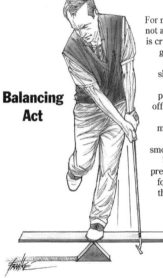

For many golfers, your balance is probably not as good as it could be. Good balance is crucial to hitting consistent and concise golf shots. Here's a practice-tee drill to help sharpen up your balance. Grab a short iron (a 7-, 8- or 9-) and tee up the ball. Set up in your normal address position, then slowly lift your right foot off the ground. Now hit the shot. At first you'll probably have too much lateral movement and lose your balance. Stick with it and concentrate on making smooth, controlled swings. Try to hit the ball only 40 to 50 yards. Once you get pretty good at it, reverse feet so your left foot is off the ground. When you get to the point where you're able to hit good shots off either foot, it will be "cake" hitting the ball solidly on two feet.

Section 4:

MASTER·STROKES

NO

REVERSE PIVOT

YES

Are You In Reverse?

Many casual golfers have what is called a reverse pivot, which means your weight transfer is backward. This happens when you are trying to pivot holding the head too still. By doing this, it causes the weight to shift to the opposite side of your body, which means the weight is on the front foot instead of the back foot at the top of the swing. Free up your swing by allowing the head to move a bit during the backswing. The body will coil better and the head will be behind the ball, which means more distance and better control.

Practice Drills

Rubber Disks

As you age, your balance might not be quite as good as it was when you were younger. A great way to restore your feel of balance and also help with the correct turn sequence is to use these soft and flexible rubber disks. The key is getting on the disks and getting balanced. Then try slowly swinging the club back to the top. If you tilt or lift during the swing, you will quickly get out of balance due to the uncertain support of these disks. The better you can stay in balance will have a direct result in a better, more effective turn. This drill also helps you have more awareness of exactly what your body and feet are sensing, which provides you the feedback for improvement. Use this drill often to assist you with improving your balance and making a more efficient turn.

Step It Up For Spring

The "step/baseball" drill teaches the correct sequence of motion, rhythm, timing and balance, just like a baseball player stepping toward the pitcher as he triggers himself ready to drop the bat down and into the path of an oncoming pitch. When the ball is approaching, the player picks up his front foot and steps toward the mound. To practice this drill: (1) Put your feet close together, swing back and turn away. (2) Just before you reach the top, lift your front foot and step toward the target. (3) Turn back, dropping your arms and club, and swing through to the finish. The club will fall into place, reacting to the shift and turn of the body.

Like a baseball batter, this action is the trigger to unleash a powerful swing. You can envision and feel how natural and smooth this type of hitting action is, a flowing swing tempo that translates into crisp ball striking.

Practice Drills

MASTER·STROKES

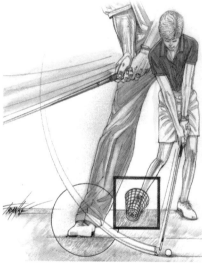

Foot In The Bucket

A range basket is a perfect tool to slow down the overactive lower body. Place your back foot in the basket. As you are coming into the ball on the downswing, you will feel a more stable base, and the arms will have a better chance of getting back in front of the body. If the lower body is too active, it forces the arms to lag too far behind, resulting in a slapping motion at impact. This drill creates a better sequence of motion so that when you hit shots without the bucket, your body and arms will work more together.

MASTER·STROKES

Your Downswing Has Become Too Shallow!

How do you know? You're hitting a lot of hooks. When you're not hitting hooks, you're hitting behind the ball or catching it thin. Even a "slot swinger" can get too shallow on the way back to the ball. "The slot" is a position and path that all pros, after the transition from their backswing, drop their club into while delivering the clubhead to impact.

They get "under plane" and swing "inside out." The ideal swing arc, what I call the "power line path," is inside, down the line and then back inside.

To get back on plane and into the slot, try this drill:

1) Address an imaginary ball, swing to the top of your backswing and stop.

2) Swing down at 60 percent speed and stop with hands hip high at the halfway-down position (turn hips, don't slide; flatten clubshaft, not arms). Check that the shaft is parallel to the target line and not pointing to the right, with the toe pointing up. Rehearse this move until you always end up in this position.

3) Swing to the halfway-through position and stop with the shaft pointing toward the target. Again, the clubshaft should sit on the parallel target line, with the toe pointing up.

Repeat as many times as necessary until your hands and arms work in concert with the shaft. You're back "on line."

MASTER·STROKES

Glue Your Right Elbow

On the downswing, glue your right elbow to your right side. Having your right elbow in this position, tucked into your right side, will help prevent the "over the top" **SLICE SWING**. It also helps keep the club on plane and the clubface square to that plane. This "delivery position," as I call it, is a key to any swing. It contributes to square, on-line contact as well as increased clubhead speed. Fast and square at impact will **"SMASH"** the ball long and straight.

MASTER·STROKES

Weighted Club Drill

Many amateur golfers lose swing speed by dumping their club on the way down, meaning their hands release the club too early. A great training exercise used by many tour pros is swinging a weighted club (from an 8-ounce doughnut to a very heavy 2- to 3-pound club). After swinging back to the top, they stop, feel the weight, then start down very slowly and stop halfway down (9:00 clubshaft position, pointing behind with hands off right thigh). This is practicing a "delayed hit" and helps them train to keep the clubhead back before unleashing through impact, which generates tremendous clubhead speed. Another drill is making nice, slow swings all the way through to finish. After swinging a weighted club, a normal club will feel like a feather and will increase your swing speed.

Practice Drills

Shifty Golfers – Right Foot Up!

Many golfers make poor contact and suffer a
loss of power due to their lack of proper weight shift.
Their weight needs to be fully transferred onto their
left or front foot on the downswing. This drill will
help you get back that feeling of having your weight
where it belongs. Place an object that is 8 to 10
inches tall on the practice tee. An upside-down
range ball basket will do fine.

Set up to hit iron shots while placing your right
or back foot up on the basket, but with nearly all
your weight on your forward foot. Now start hitting
shots from this position. Be conscious of feeling your
weight distributed forward at con-
tact. With practice, this drill
should feed into your regular
swing out on the course.

weig
left

Go Toe To Toe

If you can keep your clubface square in relation to the path of your swing for as long as possible, it will be far easier to be square at impact. Here's a great way to practice being square. Take your longest iron that has the flattest clubface and make practice swings with the clubshaft moving back and through, going no farther up than parallel to the ground in either direction. When your clubshaft reaches this parallel position in the backswing or follow-through, check to see if the toe is pointing straight up (90 degrees). You don't want the clubface angled in front of you or behind you. Practice the correct "toe up" position on either side of the ball until it becomes second nature. You'll be square through impact, producing nice, straight shots.

Toe
Up

Toe
Up

Square

No Shanks!

The shank is one of the most dreaded shots in golf. This is when you contact the ball off the club's hosel, causing it to squirt wildly out to the right.

If shanking the ball is one of your golfing nightmares, here's a drill to help rid you of this nemesis. Bring a 1- or 2-foot section of a two-by-four to the practice tee. Lay the board down on your target line. Place the ball next to the board and assume your address position. There should be no more than 1 inch between the toe of the club and the board. Start off by making half-swings while concentrating on keeping the clubhead from contacting the board. This keeps the hosel far enough out to ensure not shanking. As you continue to make shank-free contact, gradually increase to three-quarter swings, then finally full swings. Do this drill until you ingrain the proper setup distance between you and the ball, so your contact is "sweetly" centered on your clubface. Say "no shank you" to shanks!

Feet Together

One of the most important components of a good, solid swing is balance. It's also the most overlooked. Without good balance, hitting the ball squarely on a consistent basis is just not going to happen. You simply cannot get back to square at impact if you're moving all over the place.

The best drill to improve your balance is hitting balls with your feet together. Stand with the insides of your feet touching, take your driver and make a swing. If you swing too hard and overshift your weight going back or following through, you'll fall over. Now try the same drill using a 9-iron, making smooth three-quarter swings. Notice how much better your balance is. When you play your next round, use this swing action with your normal stance and all your clubs. You will hit much more consistent shots. Make it a routine to include this drill in your practice sessions.

Slam The Door On Your Slice

Imagine you're slamming a door closed;
imagine your clubface is that same door.
That "shut door/clubface" will hit a straight
shot. If that door/clubface did not close all
the way, the ball will slice. That's a very
common problem for the vast majority
of amateurs. They push (straight right)
or slice (curve right) their long shots.
Your offseason homework is to practice
acting out the proper impact position so
you ingrain this correct move into your
swing. When you get to the driving range
this spring, you must make the door slam
the instant your clubface reaches the ball.
"Slam the door" aggressively, and you'll
find that the ball will jump off your clubface
with more force, and on target.

MASTER·STROKES

Nothing But A Noodle

To learn the correct shape of the swing and especially get to a better impact position, this is a great drill. Take a simple swimming noodle and place it on a broken shaft and place the shaft in the ground far enough away so that you don't hit it during the takeaway. The key is that as you are swinging down to the ball, you are delivering the club to a more inside path, thus missing the noodle and making solid contact with the ball. You will feel a much easier swing as the club travels more under and gives you a feel you can repeat.

Step Up

Where did your old distance go? If you're a golfer who is hitting the ball shorter than you used to, you might think it's gone forever, just like the good old days. Not necessarily true. Your problem could be as simple as an improper weight shift, leaving too much weight on your back foot. To maximize distance, you need clubhead speed at and through impact. This is achieved by transferring your weight from back to front on the downswing. Here's a drill to help get back that athletic swing, and with that, restored distance. Get out to the practice tee with an iron and a bucket of balls. Start by hitting some nice, easy controlled shots. As you hit through the ball, try lifting your rear foot so that you end up in the finished position standing on only your front leg. At first this might be difficult, but just keep hitting balls until you can finish up in a nice, balanced finish with "a leg up."

Uphill Battle

Many casual golfers struggle with the problem of hitting their shots off the heel of the clubface. It usually results in a weak and faded shot to the right. A great drill to help solve this problem is to hit a bucket of balls off a "ball above your feet" lie. Place a ball 4 to 6 inches up a slope above your feet. In essence, you're creating a "hook lie." Hitting a ball on an uphill slope forces the club to turn in, with the toe closing on an inside path to the ball. That helps create a "clubface square at impact" path, rather than the dreaded outside-to-inside "slice" path.

The Pinch Drill

The pinch is a small swing in which you squeeze or pinch the golf ball off the turf and then hold the swing right after impact. It teaches you where you need to be at impact and what it should feel like.

You make a small swing back and – BOOM – you pinch the ball, then hold the finish in a very short position. You want a flat left wrist (no flipping of the hands – biggest power leak you could have) and the club pointed back to center. The left (lead) arm must be connected to the upper left part of the body from the middle of the upper left arm up, not from the elbow up. I also insist that the clubhead is stable and below the hands. The hips, not the hands, generate the power. To do this drill correctly, you need good footwork, good weight shift and good rotation to achieve solid impact. You will be stunned how far the ball goes and how solid it feels.

Time To Fold Up

Many amateurs have bad swings simply because the swings are incomplete. They fail to release the club through the impact zone, holding on too long, with their left arm extended, and trying to keep the face square down the target line. It actually prohibits the club from rotating properly from open to square to closed through impact, sending the ball out to the right. To correct this, practice folding both arms at the elbows shortly past impact, as opposed to keeping the left arm straight well into the follow-through. Finish with your chest pointing at the target and with both elbows close together and folded, so that the clubshaft falls directly behind and across your back. Once you get your timing down and complete your swing, your shots will fly straighter and farther.

FOLD!

Split It To Really Hit It!

Did you hit the ball straight right, "blocking" it, last season? It could be you're not releasing your hands and arms through the ball and after impact. If so, the "split-hand drill" would be great for you this off-season. It teaches the correct rotation of your forearms during the swing, in which your right forearm crosses freely over your left through the impact zone, squaring and then closing the clubface. Take your stance with a middle iron and grip it normally, holding the clubshaft horizontally in front of you. Then slide your right hand to the bottom of the grip, so there's a space of 3 to 4 inches between your hands. Next, swing the clubhead back and forth in front of you. Notice how the right forearm crosses over the left as you swing through, properly releasing arms, hands and clubhead. Try this drill for a couple of minutes each day, then, weather permitting, take it to the driving range and hit some practice balls.

You'll feel a freer arm swing, with more extension, and you'll watch your shots fly straight, high and far.

Hold Your Finish

Good balance is essential to great ball striking. Balance is the most overlooked aspect of the golf swing. It's impossible to make square, solid contact through impact if you're off-balance. Here's a great, simple tip to add to your practice routine that will help improve your balance. Take your normal swing (best with your driver or long irons) and try to hold your finish, nice and straight, for a three-count. You will find that this is not as easy as it sounds. In order to have good-enough balance to hold your finish, you must develop a smooth, flowing downswing motion.

Many golfers end up off-balance due to lurching or excessive lateral motion. This is usually caused by trying to hit the shot too hard. When you're able to hold your finish position for a three-count after swinging, you will have a nice, smooth swing.

Next, try hitting with your eyes closed. If you can hit the ball and finish balanced with your eyes closed, you have a pretty sweet swing.

Balance

Practice Drills

MASTER·STROKES

Wind-Tunnel Test

Want the truth? If you really want to know your swing and your ability to make shots, practice hitting into the wind. Why? Hitting into the wind will magnify any errors in your ball striking. For example, a shot that fades 10 yards to the right without wind will slice 20 yards into a firm breeze. That same exact shot downwind will have decreased spin, allowing the ball to fly nearly straight and farther, giving you false information. So, hitting practice shots into the wind will teach you to be more precise. You will have to hit the ball more squarely in order to make it fly straight due to the extreme sensitivity. Also, you'll find a smooth swing will bore the ball through the wind better than trying to kill it.

Section 4:

140

MASTER·STROKES

Off-The-Wall Wedges

The wall drill helps check if your pitching wedge backswing is correct. Too many amateurs jerk the clubhead back inside too quickly and too flat around their body. Address the ball with the wall behind you so your heels are about a foot away. Next, swing back. If the club hits the wall, you know that you are probably overusing your hands instead of letting the club be directed back and up more with your arms and shoulders. The weight of the clubhead should be automatically hinging your right wrist once you reach the halfway point in the backswing. If you don't feel this happening, you must consciously hinge your right wrist at this halfway point. Repeat this until you get used to swinging the wedge on the proper plane. Done correctly, you will not hit the wall.

Practice Short Game

If you're a golfer who now finds himself with more time to practice, here's a way to make that practice more fun. Set up the 'Practice Short Games,' either by yourself or, better yet, competing with your playing buddies.

First – Basic Chip: Play 10 chip shots from just off the green, 35-50 feet from the hole. Score 5 points for a hole-out, 2 points for shots within 2 feet and 1 point for shots within 4 feet.

Second – Short Pitch and Run: Play 10 shots from 10-15 yards off the green, 60-90 feet from the hole. Score 10 points for a hole-out, 2 points for within 4 feet and 1 point for within 8 feet.

Third – Greenside Bunker Shot: Play 10 shots from a normal lie, 40-60 feet from the hole. Score 20 points for a hole-out, 2 points for within 6 feet and 1 point for within 12 feet.

Count your total points, have fun and always try to top it next time. You'll get real "short sharp."

MASTER·STROKES

Chipping Rules

In "CHIPPING 101," we talked about keeping your left or lead wrist firm through impact. Allowing your left wrist to break down lets the clubhead move ahead of the hands. This usually results in a scuffed or fat shot, with a big bogey on the hole. Here's a great drill to help you get it right. Put your watch on or use a rubber band, and slip a 12-inch ruler under the band so the ruler runs from the knuckles to the forearm. Hit some practice chip shots. If you feel your knuckles press against the end of the ruler, you'll know your left wrist is breaking down. Keep practicing until there is no contact between your knuckles and the ruler. You will be back on course with a great chipping stroke, making firm, consistent contact, and you'll be dropping birdies instead of bogeys.

Practice Drills

One-Armed-Bandit Chipper

Many casual golfers "break down" on their chip shots. That is, the left wrist flips or scoops at the ball. Here's a great drill to help this problem. Take the club in your left hand only. Place the ball in the center or toward the back of your stance (delofting the club). Place 60 percent of your weight on the front foot. Lean the shaft forward at address. Position your head in front of the ball. Backswing and follow-through should be equal distances. Keep your lower body still on the backswing, with very little leg action as well on the forward swing.

At impact, keep your left arm and club in a straight line. Your left wrist is to remain flat and firm. With left-arm-only practice, struggling chippers will get the correct feel.

No

LEAD
WRIST
FIRM

FRANKE

MASTER·STROKES

Bring Your Handkerchief To Practice

One of the most common errors in practicing short shots for amateurs is a lack of focus on the landing area. A great drill for this is to place a handkerchief flat on the landing area of your intended target. By landing the ball on the handkerchief you will develop better touch and feel for your chipping and pitching. To get the most out of this, use different-length shots, and vary your club selection so that you don't get bored hitting to the same target. More importantly, you'll learn the feel for more shots.

Practice Drills

Up And Down

The best way to increase your up-and-down (chip, pitch or sand shot and then one putt) percentage is to have a contest with a golfing buddy or spouse. Try this competition: Have each player hit three shots from a selected location, and then putt out the best and worst shot and total the score. Consider a score of five strokes per hole as par. Let the winner of the previous hole select the next shot, or alternate the selection. So that you'll be better able to handle any situation you encounter on the course, drop the ball and play it as it lies.

Sand Dollars

You have probably heard the analogy of hitting two inches behind the ball when in the sand. What I see is that golfers who use this visual term tend to dig and many times decelerate the club. I like teaching the "dollar drill," because you must enter the sand at the edge of the dollar, with the object being to throw the dollar out onto the green while sand and the ball come with it. This encourages you to follow through. If you chop or dig too much, you will tear the dollar. Place the ball in the middle of the dollar, then swing under the edge of the dollar with your clubface open and, with the clubhead continuing underneath the dollar, complete your follow-through.

FACE OPEN

MASTER·STROKES

Dialing Long-Distance

Getting the distance correct on putts of 40 feet or longer is harder to do than finding an accurate line. This is especially true for golfers who have lost some touch. This drill will help.

Get out to the practice green and pick out a long downhill putt. Using three balls, intentionally roll the first ball four feet past the hole. Hit the second ball three feet short. Now that you have some feel for being long or short, try to roll ball No. 3 so that it rolls the perfect speed, stopping just a few inches past the hole. Next, try this with long uphill putts and then putts with varying speeds. If you commit to this practice, your feel on long putts will improve dramatically.

MASTER·STROKES

Putting, Down To A Tee

Some of the world's greatest players often won't putt to a hole when practicing. Instead they practice rolling their putts to a tee they've stuck into the practice green. The reason: If they're working on their stroke, or just trying to roll the ball a certain distance, they aren't interested in their ball going into the hole. They want putting mechanics to give them "pinpoint" accuracy or stroke feel and provide them correct "dialed-in" distance. Besides, later on, the hole looks massive during their round, when they're trying to sink "putts for dough."

Practice Drills

Is Your Putting Too Mechanical?

Your putts have been erratic. You just don't have the "feel" when stroking the ball.

Instead, you feel uncomfortable and stiff. You're probably struggling with too many mechanical thoughts when you are putting. Here's a cure.

Try these two drills. First, hit several putts from various distances while looking at the hole, not the ball, during your stroke. This will help you take the mechanics out of your stroke by calling on your inborn ability to assess direction and distance. Your binocular vision is made for judging direction and distance. Your eyes then send impulses to your muscles. Second, hit the same putts with your eyes closed. This will greatly increase your sense of feel and touch. Again, you must force yourself to rely on your natural instincts. Trust your instincts. They're in there – use them.

A Dime's Worth

A dime can go a long way. But that's only if you have a nice, level putting stroke. Unfortunately, some golfers don't know what that feels like. If you're one of them, that "jerky" motion you've been calling a putting stroke doesn't roll the ball true to the hole very often, does it? Here's a simple tip to help you gain that feeling. Place a dime on a flat, hard surface, standing it up on edge. Try rolling it straight. You'll find it's not that easy to do. Most likely your dime will go off to one side or the other, then fall over quickly. With practice, you will start to make adjustments that will enable you to keep that dime up and rolling straight. These adjustments will help you teach yourself a nice, level stroke, giving you that feeling of a smooth, level putting stroke. Take that feeling to the green with you and start draining putts on a regular basis.

Square Stripes

Your putting has been LOUSY! It's just killing your rounds. You're clearly not stroking your putts squarely, causing your putts to "lip out" or miss left or right.

If your ball is wobbly and not rolling with a pure end-over-end motion, here is a simple little trick to help. Get over to the practice green, taking with you a range ball with a red stripe around it. Set up with as straight a putt as you can find. Line up the ball's stripe exactly toward the hole, then hit it. Take notice of the roll – did the stripe still wobble, or did it roll perfectly end over end? Dedicate yourself to practicing, staying smooth and calm and striking your putts cleanly and precisely. You will start to roll that stripe end over end. Ingrain this "feel" into your putting regiment. Do this until you're a "putting machine" that will confidently roll a sweet ball every time you stroke that putter, and you will watch your putts drop in.

MASTER·STROKES

Aim Blame

When golfers miss short "breaker" putts that are makable, they most often blame their stroke.

The cup is 4¼ inches wide. It's actually tough to miss a short breaker putt either high or low by just mishitting it. You need to mishit the ball by more than a whole 2 inches left or right for the ball not to fall in. Faulty alignment when aiming at the spot of break is the more likely cause.

Go to the practice green with a friend and a ruler. Take your normal setup on a hole and have your friend check your alignment by sighting from behind you. He then will place the ruler in line with where your putter face is aiming (a spot where you judge the break to be, rather than the cup). Step back and see if you are actually aligning as you think you are. Do this on many holes. If you see a tendency to be off aim, this checkup should help you sense how to adjust so you will be properly aimed on short breakers in the future.

MASTER·STROKES

Living On The Edge

If your putting has been "SHAKY" in the three- to five-foot range, try this exercise to sharpen your accuracy. On the practice green, line up so that you have a flat, straight four-foot putt. However, your focus will be to drop the ball specifically into the right side of the cup. Next, drop the ball into the left side. Putts that go right into the cup's center should be regarded as a miss.

By practicing with a more specific, smaller target, your aim and stroke will both become more precise, while also achieving an improved sensitivity for ball speed. But, of course, aim for the cup's center while playing. After practicing this drill, the hole will look as big as a dinner plate.

MASTER·STROKES

Pool Shark

The difference between a great score and another pedestrian round is often the difference between making your short putts and missing them.

To help sharpen your putting game, place three balls 4 to 6 inches away from the front lip of the cup. Set up 3 to 6 feet away with another ball. Now select which ball you would like to knock in the hole with the ball you're about to putt. Think of it like playing a billiard shot. Not easy! In order for you to be able to knock all these balls in the hole, you're going to have to be a real sharpshooter. It will require a much more precise shot than you would need to sink a simple putt.

This is a fun drill that will develop your concentration, touch and precision.

Make this drill a regular part of your practice and the cup will look like a manhole cover out on the course.

Putting Feel

To prevent wrists flipping while putting, I like to use the "one hand at a time" putting drill. Get about 3 feet from the hole and then place just the left hand on the grip. Then simply stroke the ball into the cup. This drill will make you aware of what your hands are doing throughout the stroke. You can make easy corrections just by getting the proper feed back from this stroke. Change hands and repeat the drill.

MASTER·STROKES

Shut-Eye Putting

Most short putts are missed due to too much movement while putting. A great way to practice staying quiet with your entire body during the stroke is to practice putting with your eyes closed.

Line up a 3-footer as you normally would. Take a good look at the hole. Then close your eyes and stroke the putt. Hear the putt fall in – don't see it, hear it! You might be surprised to find you can make more putts with your eyes closed rather than open. This is due to the fact that when your eyes are closed, you will stay incredibly still throughout the stroke. You're now more aware of staying still and under control because you can't see. You naturally quiet yourself down. This is the feeling you need to have for consistent, rock-solid putting – quiet and under control.

LISTEN!

3'

MASTER·STROKES

Got Golf Itch?

While you're stuck inside the house looking out at snowdrifts and dreaming of spring, you could be honing your golf game. Pros sharpen their putting all the time in their hotel rooms. Practice on very thin, fast-running carpet. It will help you simulate the course experience. Avoid shag or deep, plush carpet, because it will encourage you to make your stroke too hard and long. Simply place some golf balls down on the floor and putt into the openings of water glasses set out at different distances. Or you can putt to chair legs, pretending that you need to hole the putt to win a big match. Try some long putts into the next room, if possible. You'll be sharp in the spring.

It's OK To Be Snappy

Hey golfers, don't let yourself get too rusty this offseason. Pick up a club every day and practice swinging for a while. Along with staying loose, take advantage of your free time by ingraining some more snap into your downswing. The "whoosh" drill will help add distance when your new season starts. Take an old driver and hold it upside down. Grip it in your right hand only, just above the clubhead. Position the club as you would at the top of the backswing. Now, as you swing down and through, try to make as loud a "whoosh" at impact as you can. To do so, you'll need to actively snap your right hand and forearm through the impact zone. Also, you'll generate maximum speed when you push off with your right foot and the inside of your right leg. Learn to use your right side (arm and leg) to create that extra whoosh, and you'll be hitting longer shots out on the course.

Practice Drills

Keep It Together

A major reason amateurs lack power and accuracy is that they "disconnect" their body and arms during their backswing. This means they swing their arms and club back without turning their torso. This arms-only swing will result in very weak and inconsistent shots.

Here's a great offseason drill to get you "connected" for more powerful and consistent shots next spring. Take your driver and hold it on the shaft below the grip, so that the butt of the grip is against your bellybutton. Next, make a slow-motion backswing turn, keeping the clubhead touching your stomach and between your arms. Make sure your club is straight in front of you as you turn as far back as you can. Keeping the club in front of you helps unify the motion of the arms with that of your torso. This is the "connected" feel you want. A one-piece-motion backswing lets you build maximum power for the downswing. It also leads to repetitive, and therefore consistent, contact. Repeat this drill every day to ingrain this "connected" feel into your golf swing.

ALL ARMS

Keep Sharp!

Keeping sharp in the offseason by doing coordination drills will pay off when you tee it up in the spring. Good eye/hand coordination results in more solidly hit, more accurate and more powerful shots. Do this fun drill all winter – it's a little tough at first but very beneficial. Take a ball and your driver. Hold your driver just a few inches from the neck of the clubhead with its face facing the sky. Drop the ball on the clubface and tap it upward as many times as you can. It won't be easy, but stay with it. When you get to the level of 10 straight taps in a row, reverse hands and try to get to the same level with your opposite hand. If you can achieve this level, gradually increase the distance between your hand and the clubhead, which makes the challenge even more difficult while improving your eye/hand coordination for sharp ball striking.

Practice Drills

'Mirror, Mirror On The Wall'

If inclement weather or the "offseason" won't allow you to play, this "downtime" is an excellent opportunity to get back to basics. Solid fundamentals are the foundation of a successful golf game. But many struggling amateurs have trouble due to something as simple as poor posture at address.

A common flaw is having their back too upright, causing two major problems:

1) This leads to a swing that is too flat and too much around the body.

2) The player has to reach too much with his arms, causing tension and making a perfect return of the club at impact nearly impossible.

To help correct this problem, practice "setting up" in front of a mirror at home every day. Start by flexing your knees slightly, then bend your back forward from the waist, making sure to keep your back straight. From this stance you can let your arms hang down in a natural relaxed position.

This correct posture will give your arms plenty of room to clear your body during the swing.

Dream Golf

Here's a common-sense driving-range routine to help make your practice more productive and more fun. Try the "fairways and greens" game, practicing as if you're playing your home course shot by shot. Imagine you're teeing off on the first hole. Pick out two markers at the correct distance that substitute as boundaries to the first fairway you would be facing. Now tee off with your normal club and determine whether you hit the fairway or not. Next select the club you would need to hit the green from this estimated lie. Aim for a precise target representing the flag and determine whether your shot landed on the green.

Go through your entire course by hitting all the full shots required in their normal sequence. After you walk off your make-believe 18th hole, calculate your score to see how well you did.

Practice Drills

SECTION 5:
Strategy

What goes on inside your head during a round of golf will largely determine what happens for you outside on the golf course. A round of golf consists mostly of time between shots. These tips will show you how to put all that time to good use by thinking about ways to improve your swing and formulating strategies to lower your score.

CONTENTS

MASTER·STROKES

Seven Crucial Steps

If you think golf pros get great results just because they hit it good, you would be wrong.

They all have an analytical-approach ritual that helps them succeed repeatedly. This analytical ritual is just as important as their physical ritual.

Here are my several crucial tips that you should execute before even thinking about setting up to a golf shot.

These tips are:

1) Identify your ball.
2) Analyze the lie.
3) Check your surroundings.
4) Check wind direction and speed.
5) Identify your target line.
6) Survey the target area.
7) Determine distance

It very often will not matter how well you struck the ball if you didn't first follow a checklist like this.

Strategy

MASTER·STROKES

A Winning Attitude

Harry Vardon, one of the greats of all time, had a novel way of staying calm on the golf course. Instead of expecting perfection, he took a more realistic attitude and anticipated hitting seven bad shots per round. Instead of getting angry when he inevitably hit his first bad shot, he would simply say, only six more bad shots to go. This philosophy allowed Vardon to accept mistakes and helped him play to his potential. Try this trick for your own game by adding Vardon's seven bad shots to your handicap (for example, a 10-handicap golfer should expect 17 bad shots per round). Then start the countdown. You'll stay calm and have more fun.

MASTER·STROKES

Early-Bird Special

We have all heard that the "early bird" catches the worm. Well, the "early golfer" has the best chance of catching a good score. It goes without saying that it's never a good idea to run up to the first tee box without a practice swing. Your chances of having a good round aren't very good. Your chances of getting hurt are excellent. A good plan would be getting to the course 30 minutes before your scheduled start. This will allow you to do 5 minutes of stretching exercises, then hit some easy practice shots for 15 minutes (20-25 balls) and, finally, spend 10 minutes getting a feel for your putting stroke, along with hitting a few chips. You'll be off to the first tee loose, confident and ready to go low.

169   **Strategy**

It's Just A Game

Just like Tiger Woods is arguably the most competitive player today, Jack Nicklaus was the fiercest competitor of his day. Nicklaus was asked if he was still going to dinner after losing a classic battle in the British Open to Tom Watson. He answered, "Of course we're going, it's just a game." Take the lead from Jack; keep a round of golf in perspective. It is only a game – a game and a walk to be enjoyed. Missing a putt or slicing your drive into the trees isn't the end of the world as we know it. It's not even "doomsday."

It's OK to be competitive and intensely focused, but keep it positive so you don't suck the reason for "playing" out of it. Enjoy the game and "a walk not spoiled." You'll play better.

Join The Arm-y?

Here's a simple little swing thought that will help amateurs generate more clubhead speed through the impact zone. As you start your downswing, try to make your right or rear forearm catch up to and touch the inside of your left forearm. You will never actually accomplish this, but the attempt to catch up will cause you to speed up your entire right side through the ball as quickly as you possibly can. This action will translate into maximum clubhead speed. Practice this swing thought image with full-swing shots. You'll find yourself putting a lot more zip into your shots.

MASTER·STROKES

One Is The Loneliest Number

One is the loneliest number, but it's the right number if we're talking swing thoughts. The golf swing happens so quickly, you can't possibly think of all the many different concerns. Thoughts of backswing, transition, downswing and finish are way too crippling. Simply put, less is more. One swing thought is just right. Make it a simple one. For example, "take it back slowly," "balanced finish," "hit down on the ball." These are simple and positive. Pick one.

MASTER·STROKES

Practice Rounds Count, Big-Time

We are completely speaking from experience here. If you have a big match or even a fun tournament coming up, take a day to get in a practice round on the golf course you will be playing. This sounds like a "duh," but most amateur golfers never do it.

Just having the confidence that you are properly prepared will help you. More importantly, any blind spots or local knowledge can really bang up your scorecard when you're unaware of it. Of course, having an idea about the green you're about to land on is huge in your shot strategy and approach.

This obvious but smart extra effort will pay off big.

173   **Strategy**

MASTER·STROKES

I'LL HAVE A NO. 5 (LIGHT GRIP), PLEASE

How many times have we told you, tension is a killer! It has an incredible ability to undo all of your preparations and make swinging the club difficult to execute with balance and rhythm.

If you feel the slightest sensation in tenseness or rigidity in your shoulders, back away, take a deep breath and exhale very slowly. Do this a few times, if needed, and get back into your stance. Notice how some pros wiggle their arms like wet noodles or waggle their club before hitting? Keep the "tension free" feel right down to your hands, and your grip pressure at about a 5 or less on my scale of 1 to 10. Favoring a light grip will help keep tension from creeping into your swing, resulting in the longest shots you will ever hit.

Light Grip #5

MASTER·STROKES

The Face Of The Club

When it comes to playing tennis, the face of the racket is very large, unlike a golf club, which is much smaller. If you learn what the clubface should be doing throughout the swing, it makes the ball striking much better. For example, golfers tend to think of so many things in their swing that they lose focus on what the clubface is doing. Picture your clubface being the size of a tennis racket, and as you get to impact, visualize the face of the club making square contact in line with your target. Remember, clubface to the target and swing through.

175

MASTER·STROKES

You Have To Travel Wide And Far For Power!

If you would like to build a really powerful swing this coming season, you will need to increase the arc width of your swing. This includes both your take-away and your follow-through. Here's how: In your take-away, reach your arms away from your body as far as possible, trying for full extension. Be careful to not let your head accompany your arms on this journey (a little head movement laterally away from the target on the backswing is OK).

Also, keep your take-away low and slow – this promotes width. On the downswing, swing through the ball, making sure to extend your arms as far forward as you can, reaching toward the fairway. But once again, be careful to not allow your head to move too far forward until your arms literally pull you out of the shot to your finish.

MASTER·STROKES

Ax Man

Old-school golf teaches that a right-handed player should have his left side dominate the downswing. This means your weight should transfer quickly from your right side to your left side as you begin your downswing, with your left arm pulling your right arm down.

Here's a different approach that can help golfers looking for maximum power. Imagine you are chopping down a tree. You would want to deliver a level, powerful blow with your ax. After swinging the ax back, you wouldn't just shift your weight to your left side and pull with your left arm. You would use the strength of your entire body, including your right side, arms and shoulders, to help drive the ax deep into the tree trunk. Use this tree-chopping image to discover a newfound force that will add power to your game.

Strategy

Ball Flight Factors? Face Vs. Path

My learning experience and true understanding of ball flight and how curvature happens started on a par-3 hole on my home course. It has very steep bunkers on the right side, a hill on the left side, and the green slopes severely from right to left. I use the commonly accepted method: Aim the clubface at the target, align your body where you want the ball to start and then swing the clubhead across this target line and your body lines. This shot would start at the flag, curve to the right and land in the bunker. Then I discovered, after reading an early Mike Hebron book, that the face angle has a much more dominant effect on the starting direction of the ball than the clubhead path. This knowledge helped me understand why I kept ending up in the bunker. The ball was starting too close to where I was aiming, and because of my fade alignment and swing path, it was curving more than I expected. When attempting a shot like this, adjust your aim by factoring in the dominance of the face angle.

Par-3 Danger Zone!

Not taking your par-3s as seriously as you take the par-5s can be very damaging to your round. A double-bogey 5 on a 3 is just as bad as a 7 on a 5. You often see golfers who don't plan their par-3s correctly take one or more double bogeys on par-3 holes each round.

Very often, par-3 flags are well-guarded by hazards, but those pin placements usually leave you with plenty of green away from the flag to shoot at. If your tee shot calls for laser accuracy with a 9-iron, think about how many times you can pull that off. Forget about the flag. Aim for the safe, meaty section of the green, even if this leaves you with a 40-footer. You'll make plenty more pars with this approach.

Draw/Fade 101

Draw Tee it high, swing in-to-out.

To promote a draw, take a slightly closed stance and tee the ball a little higher. Align the leading edge of your clubface directly at your target. Gripping a touch lighter will help you release the club, which closes the face. Be deliberate at the top of the swing to give the club time to drop to the inside. Your swing shape should be in-to-out through impact. The through-swing is like hitting a big forehand in tennis, with a full rotation of the hands. The path caused by your closed body alignment combined with the square club-face will supply the desired right-to-left side spin to the shot.

CLUB FACE SQUARE TO TARGET LINE

Fade Tee it low, swing out-to-in.

To set up a fade, take a slightly open stance and tee the ball a little lower. Align the leading edge of your clubface directly at your target. Grip a touch firmer to hold off the release through impact and keep the face open. I waggle the club along my stance line to preset an out-to-in swing. Make your normal swing, keeping the clubhead low through impact and your left wrist firm. The path caused by your body alignment combined with the square clubface will supply the desired left-to-right side spin to the shot.

Section 5:   **180**

MASTER·STROKES

Provisional Play

When you hit your ball out of bounds or you lose your ball, you must go back to the spot of your original stroke and play another ball at a penalty of one stroke. This means you add an extra stroke to your hole's score. For example, if you hit your tee shot clearly out of bounds, you will re-tee and hit another shot that would be counted as your third shot (this includes your first lost-ball stroke and your added penalty).

1ST SHOT

PROVISIONAL

Too many golfers assume they will find their wayward shot so they don't hit a "provisional" or second shot. When they don't find it, which is normally the case, they must go all the way back to the tee. Add this to the search time and we have a big delay. So if you have any doubt about finding your ball, always hit a provisional ball from the same spot. Remember, under the rules you can never drop a ball near where you think the lost or out-of-bounds ball came to rest.

Strategy

Hole High

Believe it or not, Tour pros are often more concerned about getting the correct distance than the accuracy of their approach shots. That's because an incorrect club selection can result in a putt of 30 to 45 feet or more and can be the difference between making a birdie and a bogey. Naturally, the key to getting hole high is knowing exactly how far you hit each club. And that valuable information can be obtained easily with today's launch monitor technology. Once you know the maximum and average carry distance for every club in your set, you can create a handy pocket guide that you can refer to on the course. Your scores will surely drop when your approach shots settle hole high.

'Macho, Macho Man'

Confidence is always good in sports, and sometimes an aggressive attitude is needed, but when it comes to trying to "nuke" your short irons like the pros to make you feel "macho," it's a bad idea. Amateur and senior golfers can't let their egos get the better of them by trying to prove they can hit a pitching wedge from 140 yards or a sand wedge from 120. Even if they can reach the target from these distances (and they almost surely can't), shots that require an all-out swing are rarely accurate. So instead of having a disastrous hole trying to recover from a hazard or out of bounds, make it a rule to never swing with more than 85 percent effort when hitting your 8-iron, 9-iron, pitching wedge or sand wedge. Always choose the club that you know you can easily and confidently hit the needed distance. You will hit your short approach shots consistently close to the flag for a macho low score.

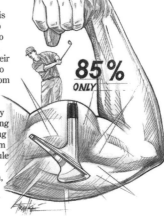

Strategy

The Long And The Short Of Altitude

If you travel to play golf or take your clubs on business trips, you need to be aware of altitude changes. The golf ball will fly different distances at different altitudes. If you are going on vacation in the mountains but normally live and play at sea level, you can expect the thinner mountain air to carry your ball about 10 percent farther than normal. Instead of hitting your 8-iron an expected 130 yards, the same struck ball will fly 146 yards at high altitudes. So make adjustments in your club selection accordingly. The opposite is also true. If you normally live and play in high altitudes and vacation near the ocean, expect your ball to not fly as far as it normally would. Adjust by taking at least one or maybe two clubs stronger than usual on your approach shots. For example, instead of using your 9-iron, you would choose your 8- or possibly even 7-iron due to the loss of distance.

Correct 'Miss' Wisdom

You must think one shot ahead when presented with a difficult pin position. Of course, you're hoping for that TV highlight "dream shot," but that's not likely to happen, especially for golfers whose "TV highlight reel" might be a bit thin. That's OK, here is some tested wisdom. Smart golf is hitting to a safer spot where you can still get down in two. Let's say the flag is tucked way right and protected by nasty deep bunkers and rough all around. A miss here leaves you a very difficult recovery shot. Be smart and aim to the left away from the flag to the fat part of the green. With an accurate shot, you'll leave yourself a 30-footer, which is doable. If you miss left, you'll have a long chip with plenty of clear green to work with, also doable in two. These "misses" are much easier to recover from. Plan ahead so your second shot is a simple one. You'll avoid trouble and score cards that you want to toss.

Hit Backward, Think Ahead

Like chess masters, the better golfers plan their moves while always thinking ahead. Follow this strategy by planning your shots from the flag back to the tee before you start. Take note of where the flag is placed and what part of the green would leave you the easiest putt. Then think where would be the best place in the fairway to hit your approach shot from to be in the optimal putting location. Next, consider where you should tee up in the tee box that will enable you to hit your fairway target, and what type of ball flight should you try for, if any. Having a well-thought-out plan of attack will optimize your chances to succeed instead of leaving yourself open to whatever difficulties and hazards might be waiting for you.

UPHILL PUTT

Section 5:

Adjust Club Selection On Uphill/Downhill Targets

Dramatic elevation changes on approach shots to greens must be factored in when selecting a club. Most amateur golfers fail to do this and end up overshooting or falling short of the green. Here's what needs to be considered:

When the target is steeply uphill, the upslope will cut off the downward flight of the ball earlier than normal. To a green well below, the ball's downward flight will continue farther.

Keep in mind that the longer the shot, the more you'll need to adjust. This is because the lower trajectory of the longer club will be affected more. For example, if for a level shot a 3-iron would be needed, you might need to make a two-club adjustment; but on a 9-iron shot that descends more steeply, you'll likely need one club more or less.

MASTER·STROKES

High IQ On Long Par-4s

There are a few holes out there on a course that can ruin your round. The really long par-4 is the one that usually gets you. Let's say you have a 450-yard hole with bunkers surrounding the green, and you don't happen to be a very good lob-shot player. Here's where playing smart comes in. Don't even think of leaving a lob shot over a bunker for your third shot. Instead, lay back off the tee and the approach shot. You need to use your head and play to your strengths. Leave yourself an easy, full-swing, 80- to 100-yard wedge shot at the flag. The opposite approach is fine if you're a long hitter who can also hit a soft-landing lob. Take two rips and try to get it on. The worst that can happen is you'll have to get it up and down from over a bunker. Either way, play smart so your round doesn't blow up.

MASTER·STROKES

Play Your Favorite

The key to being a good wedge player begins with preparation. Figure out your favorite distance and lay up consistently to that distance. If your favorite yardage is 100 yards and the hole is 310 yards, select a club for your tee shot that you dependably hit 210 yards. Also, don't misinterpret a "full" wedge to mean a hard wedge. A great wedge player maintains smoothness and control throughout the swing. A good wedge swing uses less leg action, a shorter body turn and less hand action than any other full swing.

Think control, not power, to stick those wedges tight to the hole. Play smart, which means comfortable, confident shots you know you can "dial in."

PLAY BACKWARDS FROM FAVORITE WEDGE

189

Smartegy

One of the best tips you can embrace to start fresh going into a new golf season is to be accepting of bogeys. Many golfers hurt their round by trying "miracle" shots that are outside their capabilities in order to save par. Let's say you mishit off the tee and your ball ends up in some deep rough, with the next shot needing to carry a hazard. What you need to keep in mind is that a bogey will not ruin your round. Be realistic – if you know that without your best shot ever you are not able to carry the ball the needed distance out of deep rough, don't bother trying the impossible. Instead, be sensible, lay up short of the hazard and try to get on the green in one stroke above regulation.

If you follow this strategy and you make no more than a bogey every time you get in trouble, the end result is that you'll end up having your most enjoyable season ever.

Risk Versus Reward

Hey, golfers, this may be the most important thing I can tell you about course management: On trouble shots, weigh the risk versus the reward. Of course, it depends on your skill level and other factors, like how much swing speed and distance you might have lost through the years. But you'll usually find that the risk far outweighs the reward. If you're deep in the woods or have a nasty hazard in front of you, be wise and take the sure bet. Set yourself up for the next shot to avoid a "big number." Laying up is almost always the wisest thing to do. If you have a poor lie in the fairway, an extreme carry that requires you hit it perfect, or your ball is buried in deep rough and Tiger Woods couldn't get it out and on the green, don't try it yourself.

Strategy

Wise Fives

Let's face it: most players can't reach a par-5 in two. Realizing this fact, you should play smart and hit a second shot that will leave you with the easiest approach to the green. Don't automatically reach for your 3-wood and hit the heck out of it as far as you can on your second shot. Hitting a really good 3-wood may leave you only 50 to 75 yards out. Now you have an uncertain, delicate, less-than-full wedge shot that will be harder to get close than your comfortable full wedge shot that you hit so well at a predictable distance. Also, let's say the pin is tucked on the right. You'll have an easier third shot if you place your second shot on the left side of the fairway. You need to analyze each second shot, considering the distance you would like to leave and the desired angle to the flag on par-5s.

TEE SHOT

100 YDS. OUT

60 YDS. OUT

BETTER APPROACH

Always Leave The Flagstick
In When Off The Green

Once and for all, let us put an end to your question. Yes, always leave the flagstick in when you are chipping or putting from off the edge of the green. No doubt! After numerous studies, it has been proven that you will be helped much more often than not when you leave the flagstick in the hole when putting or chipping from off the green. Whether you are downhill, uphill, or if it's level ground, leave it in. Accept the extra help the stick gives you. In the long run, it will help you drop more chips and putts, lowering your scores.

Test-Tube Putting Experiment

Here's a score-cutting approach for mid- to high-handicappers. Try this experiment in course strategy on your next round of golf. On all full-approach shots, aim to hit the center of the green, no matter what. Have total disregard for where the flag is located. Don't even look. Simply play a safe shot at the green's dead center and accept the putt that you will be left with. If you do land on the center of just about any green, you won't be left too far from the hole, while cutting down on the odds of finding severe trouble guarding the flag placement. If you play 18 holes using this strategy, you might be very surprised when you add up the numbers on your scorecard.

'C'mon, Make 'Em Quick'

Casual golfers who have lost confidence in their putting game will very often take forever to putt. They stand frozen over a putt, trying to "will" the ball into the hole. They desperately hope this extra time and thought will help their chances. This approach increases tension and is more likely to result in a quick, jerky stroke that misses more than it makes. You may have heard the old expression "miss 'em quick." It means it's better in the long run to assess your putt quickly, go with your first impression and make your stroke promptly rather than letting too much tension and indecision seep in. A more deliberate, instinctual "let's go" approach is more relaxed and therefore smoother. You will find over time that the attitude of "missing 'em quick" will have you "making 'em quick."

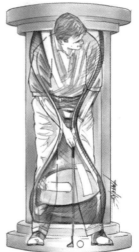

195

MASTER·STROKES

Change Up Your Putting When Struggling

Just because you have been putting a certain way for years doesn't mean you shouldn't be open to change. If it's broke, fix it! The next time you watch golf on television, pay close attention to the differences and similarities of putting styles among the players. You will see, for example, that some players take a wide stance, while others keep their feet close together. You will also see that on short putts, nearly all players keep their eyes directly over the ball. Look and learn, and then go experiment.

EYES DIRECTLY OVER BALL

WIDE

NARROW

SECTION 6:
Swing Basics

Before you move onto the particulars of specific clubs and swings required to be effective in your short game, you need to revisit the basics of a good golf swing, including how to hit the ball further so you're more often using short irons instead of the trickier longer irons. And being one of the more complex movements in sport, the golf swing involves a lot of basics.

CONTENTS

Basic Grip SEQUENCE

1) Place upper handle across left hand from base of forefinger to heel pad. Wrap up with thumb on right side of handle.

2) Wrap right-hand fingers over left forefinger and lower handle, forming unified grip with right thumb on left side of handle. "V's" formed by thumbs point to right shoulder.

Section 6:

MASTER·STROKES

Grip Lightly Or Grip Tightly?

One person's tight grip could be another person's light grip. Establish a numbering system, such as 1 through 10, where 1 is a light grip and 10 is a firm grip. Squeeze your club lightly and call that a "1"; then increase the tightness of your grip incrementally from "1" to "10" so that you recognize 10 different levels of grip strength. Having a feeling associated with each number helps you gauge proper grip pressure. A lighter pressure, 3 or 4, promotes a release (draw), while a tighter pressure, 6 or 7, hinders a release (fade). Most golf shots should be hit with a number 4 or 5 grip pressure.

Lock 'Em Up!

The most commonly used grip is the overlap grip. This grip has the little finger of your right hand overlapping behind the index finger of your left hand. This is fine unless you have short, stubby fingers. It would be difficult for the little finger to stay in its "overlapped" position. It may pull away at or after impact, affecting your ball-striking control. If you have short fingers, consider the "interlock" grip. (It works for Jack Nicklaus and Tiger Woods.) This inserts your right little finger underneath the left index finger, knitting the fingers together a bit more securely.

Of course, any change to your game should first be taken out to the practice tee to get the feel of it. Also be aware that a different grip is likely to cause some slight changes in your ball flight, so practice to learn what to expect out on the course.

Be Square

We know gripping the club correctly is one of the critical components to hitting the ball well.

Here's a surefire way to make sure you have a great grip. Use your imagination to envision that your grip is square rather than round. A square-shaped grip would have four sharp corners. Put your left hand on the grip, placing your left thumb on the RIGHT top corner. Now, place your right hand on the club so that your right thumb is resting on the top LEFT corner of the grip. This positioning of your thumbs fits your right palm nicely over the left thumb, making your hands feel like a true unit. Use this positioning for both the "interlocking" and "overlapping" grips. A solid grip will help your clubs be "square" at impact for straighter shots.

Let It Rip With A New Grip

I see a lot of great players with widely varying grips. So if you're a senior with painful arthritis, it might be helpful for you to change your interlocking or overlapping grip to the old 10-finger/baseball grip. This puts all four fingers of the right hand directly on the handle. Hopefully this will be more comfortable.

I've never felt the grip is the most important factor in a golf swing. I believe that the body motion is more important. That's not to downplay the importance of a good grip. The club should always be held more in the fingers, and the hands should be in a neutral attitude.

As a self-check, look to see that the **"V"** formed by your left thumb and forefinger points toward your right shoulder. The **"V"** formed by your right thumb and right forefinger should point toward your left shoulder.

NOTE: The 10-finger grip is good if you tend to slice, because it allows the right hand to be more dominant, which in turn allows you to more easily square the clubface at impact.

Section 6:

Where's The Wear?

Golfers who do not maintain control of their club throughout the swing will suffer a loss of accuracy and distance. Lost control could come from something as simple as where you place your grip in your hands. Golfers have much better control if they hold the club more in their fingers. Take a look at your glove. If your glove is wearing out at the heel, you are holding the club too much in your palm. This causes the grip to move around in the hand during the swing (lost control), creating friction and causing the glove to wear out on this spot. To regain lost accuracy and distance, be sure your grip placement of the club is more into your fingers.

Not IN PALM!

GRIP IN FINGERS

Swing Basics

MASTER·STROKES

Aim Clubhead First, Body Second

Often I see golfers take their time carefully aiming their body, then lastly and haphazardly aim the most important element involved: their clubface. I believe it's much more effective to first and foremost aim your clubface. That is, when you approach your golf ball, go ahead and be very precise in aiming the clubhead to your intended target. Then, after you have aimed the clubface, align your body accordingly. This is a more reliable way of being certain the club is aimed squarely on target.

Knee Flex Check

Poor posture because of improper knee flex is a big reason for many amateurs hitting bad golf shots. They might be pretty good athletes who potentially have a good swing, but this simple address problem is hurting them. They're either too stiff in the legs, making it hard to get down to the ball at impact, or they bend the knees too much, so their weight is back on their heels. Here's a great "flex check": Get a buddy to look at your address position from behind the target line. You should flex your knees just enough so that an imaginary line drawn from your rear end down to the ground should fall just outside the back of your heels. If the line falls well behind the back of your heels, reduce your knee flex; if it falls at or in front of your heels, adjust your posture by flexing your knees a little more.

JUST BACK OF HEELS

Swing Basics

Find Your Ball Position 101

Here's a simple, no-nonsense formula to help you find the right spot to position the ball in your stance. Go to a soft field with an iron club. Take your normal setup, then swing so you take a noticeable divot. Notice where the divot lies in relation to your feet. For short and middle irons, play the ball 1 inch behind where the divot starts, so you make contact while the club is still descending. For long irons and fairway woods, play it one more ball width forward, so you make contact at nearly the bottom of the swing. With a teed-up driver, move it one more ball width forward, so you connect as the club is just beginning to ascend from its lowest point.

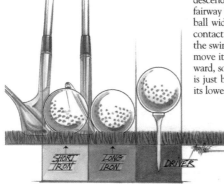

Ball Position

Ball position is where you place the ball in relation to your feet and swing center. It's vital for solid contact, the right trajectory, direction and distance.

It's ludicrous to think you can play all shots from one ball position in your stance. With a driver, the ball should be teed up opposite the inside of your left heel or instep so you catch it just after the bottom of your swing arc. Fairway woods are played slightly farther back in your stance. For long and middle irons, place the ball another inch farther back. Short irons and wedges should be played in the middle or slightly back of the middle of your stance. This positioning makes it easier to hit down on all iron shots and easier to hit from the inside, producing the desirable slight draw (right-to-left ball flight).

Swing Basics

MASTER·STROKES

Don't Reach! It's Impolite

Amateurs and seniors are much more likely to stand too far from the ball at address as opposed to standing too close to it. This is even more common when they are using a driver or long iron. They tend to reach for the ball when they set up, creating an almost straight, continuous line from their shoulders down their arms and right down the clubshaft. This is a very tense attitude. A proper attitude is for your arms to hang rather relaxed, placing your hands roughly below your head, forming a distinct angle between your arms and clubshaft (not a straight line).

An old adage that all clubs should be a "hand's width" away from your body is not correct. The club in your hand should determine how far your hands are away. With short irons, the hands will be closer. As each of your clubs increases in length and each lie is progressively flatter, the hands will move farther from the body.

MASTER·STROKES

NO SHANK YOU!

The next time you hit that sideways shot, better know as a "shank," do not panic. It isn't a mental problem, but a physical one. For starters, move an inch farther away from the golf ball. Shankers stand too close to the ball. Next, get the weight of your body back toward the heel of your foot, definitely not out on your toes. Shankers tend to lean or slump their weight too forward in their setup. And on your downswing, make sure you do not fall toward the golf ball, therefore transferring your weight out on your toes. Start off with good posture – this will help you stay balanced during your swing. A balanced swing that maintains your weight over your shoelaces will result in accurate ball striking, centered on the clubface. "SWEET!"

WEIGHT
BACK
ON
HEELS

← MOVE
BACK
AN
INCH

Frank

Swing Basics

A Good Honest Lie!

If the lie of the club is incorrect – if it doesn't sit properly on the ground – deviations in the starting direction of the ball can result. If the club is too upright, with the toe sticking up too far off the ground (1), the ball will tend to start to the left. If the club is too flat, with the heel off the ground (2), the ball will tend to start to the right. So check your lie and GO STRAIGHT!

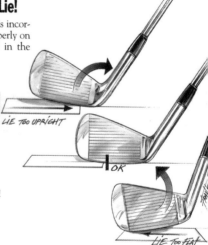

LIE TOO UPRIGHT

OK

LIE TOO FLAT

Set Up For Success

Your stance for most athletic moves will have your weight evenly balanced between your feet. The same is true in golf: To execute a well-balanced swing, you need a solid base.

That being said, in golf your weight distribution doesn't have to be a perfect 50/50. Not having your weight evenly distributed can be a helpful "prelim" for the type of shot you are about to hit. For a driver/tee shot, you should set up with a little more weight on your right or rear foot than your front foot (55 percent back to 45 percent front). This helps you stay more behind the ball, so you sweep it off the tee. In contrast, for a short iron (7-, 8- or 9-) or wedge shot, you should set up with 60 percent on your front foot and 40 percent on your back foot. This will help make a descending blow to add

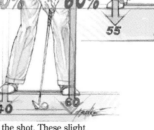

backspin and stopping power to the shot. These slight adjustments will "set you up" for more success.

Swing Basics

Slicers' Stance

If you slice the ball, you need three fundamental adjustments. First, align yourself square to the target by dropping your right foot back. Slicers tend to aim too far left or open to the target, which causes the ball to spin to the right. Second, strengthen your grip, making sure you grip the club in the fingers and not in the palm. Last, fix your posture. Keep your backside out, your knees slightly flexed and your back straight, tilted at a 45-degree angle. These three things cause more poor ball-striking than any other combination in the swing.

TARGET LINE

SQUARE

STRAIGHT
BACK

FANNY
OUT

GRIP IN
FINGERS

FLEX
KNEES

FRANKE

Slicing With Your Shoulders

Many high handicappers and senior golfers are guilty of pointing their shoulders left of target, because they leave their shoulders "open" at address. This setup produces an outside-in downswing path, resulting in a slice.

It's easy to not pick up on this, as you assume your whole body is square because you have aligned your feet square. You can see your feet, not your shoulders. Having squared feet does not guarantee your whole body is aligned properly at target.

Tour players, with the help of their coaches, pay a lot of attention to their alignment, particularly their shoulders. Practice with a buddy standing behind you holding a club across your shoulders. This will help you see if your shoulders are parallel to the target line. If not, work to get the feel of a "square" shoulder position until you can take it to the course for accurate shot making.

Swing Basics

Look Twice & Hit!

After setting up to your ball with the stance necessary for a particular shot, look intently at the target. Then glance at the ball while still jockeying your feet for balance. Repeat the look-glance procedure, then GO! I say, "Look to the target once, look to the target twice, set and go" – a proven procedure I stole from the great Johnny Revolta. Watch how many top pros instinctively use this simple pre-shot routine.

The total time for the routine is less than 30 seconds. However, the only segment that needs to be precise is after the clubhead is behind the ball and you move your feet into the correct position. Total time for the true routine is 10 seconds or less. Good players stare at the target and stay in motion. High handicappers do the opposite. They stare at the ball, with no lower-body movement. The ball is the most important thing to the poor player.

MASTER·STROKES

Sitting Down On The Job

"You lifted your head." How many times have you heard that after you or someone "topped" the ball?

Often the fault lies closer to the ground. Very often the cause is the knees straightening at impact, so that the rest of the body also is raised, along with the clubhead.

It takes some athletic ability and concentration to stay "flexed" throughout the swing.

Two Tips:

First, at address make sure your posture includes a slight, rather than a deep, knee flex. A slight flex is easier to maintain.

Second, make a conscious effort to stay "sitting" or "level" through impact. Your thighs and rear will feel slightly heavy when you retain the knee flex. Train your knees to keep the same flex throughout, and you'll find yourself hitting the ball solidly.

Swing Basics

MASTER·STROKES

Body Tension Kills The Golf Swing

Before hitting the ball, you want to be calm. Tension ties you up in knots and robs you of your natural athletic movement. If you are able, visualize the shot. Have a positive thought in your head about your swing and the outcome you anticipate. Take a free and smooth practice swing. Taking a deep breath and exhaling slowly also can help you relax your body. So chill out, and let it flow.

RELAX

Section 6:

218

Stay Connected

Many amateurs swing just using their arms, leaving their body passive. This "disconnected" swing understandably lacks power. These amateurs usually set up with their arms away from their sides, over-reaching. A good address position tip for amateurs: Set up with your elbows close to your sides. Your elbows should be soft and relaxed, rather than stretched away from the body. Prior to the start of the backswing, your elbows should be just touching your sides above the hips. As you start the club back, you should continue to feel your right elbow just barely touching your side. By keeping your elbows tucked in toward your sides, you encourage a turn of your whole body to execute the backswing. A "connected" backswing turn helps the club revolve around the body as it should, while at the same time building maximum power.

Swing Basics

Fanning The Clubface

A true death move occurs when the golfer rolls his hands or over-rotates his left forearm dramatically in the take-away. This move rolls the clubface wide open and whips the clubshaft too far to the inside. It makes your club feel heavy and off-balance. From this poor position, you have almost no chance of hitting solid golf shots.

To avoid this, move the clubhead back with no attempt to guide or rotate it, keeping the shaft between the arms. The hands are used only to maintain feel as the club rises naturally along the backward arc.

wide open

NO

YES

Section 6:

MASTER·STROKES

Stiff Arm?

"Keep your left arm straight on the backswing" – basically good advice. Any substantial bending of your left arm during the backswing can cause control problems. With that in mind, be aware that golfers who struggle to keep their left arm "board-straight" may do themselves more harm than good. A stiff left arm makes the muscles of the whole left side tight and tense, which inhibits clubhead speed and may also disrupt your swing rhythm. It's OK to have a little bend in your left elbow. So instead of a "ramrod" left arm, keep the arm extended yet relaxed, allowing it to "give" just a bit at the top of the backswing.

Swing Basics

Overextension

There is so much talk about achieving width in the backswing that it is not uncommon to see a casual golfer overextend his left arm (by overextending I mean the golfer forces the lead arm to pull away from the left shoulder).

We all have elasticity in the shoulder joint, to some degree, and by focusing too much on extension to achieve width, it's possible to disconnect from the swing path.

Establish the radius of your swing with the left arm from address.

Maintain this radius in your backswing. To do this, you're better off with a slight bend in your left elbow (underextension) during your backswing, because in the downswing that arm automatically straightens through impact.

MASTER·STROKES

It's Not All In Your Head

"You lifted your head!" How many times have you heard that after you just "topped" a shot?

It's not your head, it's your spine. We know they're connected, but your spine angle from its address position is what raised up first. Your head came with it. This happens most often when a player takes too big a backswing while trying to maximize distance.

Allowing your spine to rise will cause your clubface to arrive back at impact slightly above the ground. To stop "topping" the ball, you need to visualize your spine angle slightly forward at address. Then be conscious of rotating around it, maintaining the angle during the backswing. Getting the feel of this circular turn will be easier to do with a smooth, easy backswing, as opposed to overswinging.

Swing Basics

MASTER·STROKES

No One's Perfect

According to the "textbook," a flat left wrist (for a right-handed golfer) is preferre
throughout the swing. This is easiest to see at the top of the backswing from a down-tar
get view (on line to target).

You should know that many famous pros are not perfectly flat at the top. Some ar
"cupped," and some are "bowed."

What this tells us is that it's OK if your left wrist is in a slightly concave or a bit cuppe
position. A slightly cupped position assures tha
both hands are under the club so it's well-sup
ported (but you cannot cup so much that you
clubshaft crosses over the target line).

CUPPED

It's also OK to have a slightly con
vex left wrist position at the top, or
wrist that bends downward or is bowed a
the top. This position has the weight of the
club hanging behind the hands (off target lin
to the left), and it requires more strength an
timing to get the club back under control on th
downswing and deliver the clubhead correctly into th
impact zone. The bottom line is if you're not perfect a
the top but you're striking the ball well, stick with it. But i
you're having problems, check to see if your club position is to
cupped or bowed – it might be what's got you "off course."

FLAT

BOWED

Hammer Time

To feel the correct wrist set, you need to have a good image in your mind. Think of setting your wrists as if you were hammering a nail into a board. As you swing the club past the right knee, the club should start moving upward (by moving the hands and wrists in a cocking motion). This setting of the hands gives you more leverage in the swing and allows the club to get on the proper plane. Maintaining the wrist set throughout the backswing and during the downswing will give you a better stroke at the ball as the wrists release the club through the impact area.

Swing Basics

Shifty Character

Common advice to start the downswing is to shift your lower-body weight onto the forward foot. However, some golfers go overboard with too violent a shift toward the target, lunging their whole body forward. This causes them to lose balance and "get ahead" of the ball, so they can't deliver the clubface level and squarely through impact.

If you're having this problem, try this: When you start down, be conscious to shift your weight left, then immediately turn your left hip toward the rear instead of driving it at the target. This "shift, then turn" move will keep you in balance and will give your arms room to swing through freely and return the clubhead squarely at impact. Straighter, longer shots will follow.

Ben Hogan Motion

"The Body Swings the Arms" – Ben Hogan in "Five Lessons." Hogan epitomized the proper sequencing of downswing events: shifting (of the lower body), rotating (the core), dropping (the arms, the hands and the clubhead), keeping the shoulders back for as long as possible, and finally throwing (extending the right arm through the ball). Amateurs start the downswing with their hands and arms. Pros start the downswing with their lower body as their club is still going back. In all athletic throwing or hitting action, golf included, the lower body makes the first move forward and does it in a way that there's no specific moment at which the backswing ends and the forward swing begins. The important thing is that once you load pressure inside your back leg as you complete your shoulder coil, you're now poised to go the other way. Start your shift forward with your lower body acting as the leader for power and consistency.

Swing Basics

Hide & Seek For Straight Shots!

Amateurs most often push or slice the ball out to the right. This problem is very often caused by leaving the clubface "open" at impact. Your clubface is supposed to rotate through impact from slightly open to square, and then to closed.

Here's a simple and hopefully magical cure for this game killer.

Give yourself a simple little mental reminder to help square the clubface. Check out the emblem that's usually on the Velcro closure on the back of your glove hand. During your downswing, make a conscious effort to "hide" the emblem by releasing both hands fully (rotating them through impact) so that the back of your left hand is no longer visible. By "hiding the emblem," you'll automatically move the clubhead from an open to square position at impact. Longer, straighter shots will result.

ROTATE HAN.
THROUGH IM

Wrap It Up

The most common problem for recreational golfers is the DREADED
SLICE! A slice is caused by an open clubface. That is, the heel end of the clubface is leading the toe end into impact. A right-handed golfer's clubface is facing right (open) as the club begins to hit the ball, sending the ball spinning
clockwise out to the right. We like square impact. Square means the leading
edge of the clubface is at 90 degrees to target line. The clubface is only square
for a brief moment. The face should rotate through impact, fanning from an
open to a closed position. The feeling a golfer
should have is as if he is wrapping the
clubface around the ball, with the toe
outpacing the heel of the club. The
timing of when the face is square
needs to be learned through
practice.

Swing Basics

Keep Your Level Head Behind The Ball

"Show me a player who doesn't move his head, and I'll show you someone who can't play." – Harvey Penick, famous golf teacher.

How often have you heard the advice "Keep your head still!" and "Don't move your head!"? How famous is the person who told you that? Don't take it too seriously.

During the golf swing, your head should turn away, pivoting about 25 degrees, and move back level and slightly to the right. It has to in order to have free, athletic backswing action and good shoulder turn. That being said, you still need to make sure your head doesn't move too much. Your head, after turning away on the backswing, should go back to the address position, not any farther and not ever in front of the ball. Just like at address, your head must be behind the ball, with your left arm and shaft in a straight line, and with a flat left wrist. Allowing your head to move too far forward will have you hitting very thin, "topped" shots, resulting in "ground balls."

MASTER·STROKES

The Nineties Are Tougher Than The Seventies

I'm talking about shoulder turn, not age. The amount that you are able to pivot your shoulders is negotiable and depends on your personal flexibility in both your upper body and your hips. We watch tour pros go as far as 95 degrees. Don't be concerned if the amount your shoulders turn on the backswing is less than 90 degrees. Going past the point your flexibility and physical attributes allow will cause more problems than benefits. The fact that we don't use a full backswing when we chip or pitch the ball is evidence that the length of the backswing is not mandatory to effectively swing the club.

95°

70°

Swing Basics

MASTER·STROKES

Clock The Ball

Most golfers, when imagining a clock on the ball, think they should hit it at the 3:00 position (that's the right-side center as you look down). But golfers who think 3:00 is the ideal spot to make contact don't understand impact and separation, a topic that is almost never talked about. The correct answer is not 3:00, but rather closer to the 4:00 position. The reason for this is the club is rotating from slightly open to square through impact. The clubface contacts the inner quadrant of the ball, compresses on the face for a split second, and then comes off the face at a different position, ideally at 3:00, producing a straight shot.

Timing is everything.

Hey Fatso!

Nobody wants to hear that, especially on the golf course. Fat in golf is B-A-D! It means you've chunked it – you have struck the ground first, and too much of it, before your clubface made contact with the ball. This horrible shot goes nowhere, of course, losing almost all of its energy in the turf. The cause of these FAT shots is leaning out too far on your toes. The best way to avoid getting fat is altering your posture. Start at address by setting up with your weight over the middle of your feet. You need to be conscious of this feeling of where your weight is from front to back in your stance. Think middle – not too much heel and not too much toe. Then be certain to maintain this weight distribution throughout your backswing and downswing. Avoid falling out on your toes toward the ball. Well-balanced feet will lead to better ball striking.

WEIGHT ON MIDDLE OF FOOT

STAY OFF TOES

Swing Basics

Don't Get Off At The Wrong Stop!

Many golfers get "ball bound." This is the habit of swinging the club at the ball rather than through the ball. This tendency creates a quick, jerky action in which the clubhead is actually slowing down as it makes contact. The ball should not be your clubhead's destination. On all full shots, you should not fixate on hitting the ball. Instead, you should be thinking of making a free-flowing, full swing that happens to hit the ball as you're halfway through your swing. The golf ball is simply an object in the way of your swing path. Imagine a beach ball out in front of you that you would like to playfully hit as far as you can. This approach will generate maximum clubhead speed along with square contact.

Lighten Up Your Grip

Hey, golfers, looking for more distance? What kind of question is that? Of course, everybody is.

A simple way of getting some has nothing to do with swing or equipment. It's in your grip.

Too many "uptight" golfers are squeezing their grips into dust. An overtight grip restricts freedom of movement in your hands, wrists, arms and shoulders. This will keep you from reaching the speed you're capable of. All that's needed is to hold the club tight enough to assure that it doesn't slip or wobble during the swing. That means very light pressure at address and during the backswing. As your club speeds into the downswing, your grip pressure will increase as needed to keep control of the club, without your even knowing it. Grip easy, swing relaxed.

Get rid of that "vise grip" to add untapped power.

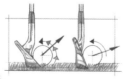

Flight Test

Ball flight can sometimes be very misleading, causing high-handicap golfers to think they are doing different things with different clubs. Many of these amateur golfers are satisfied with their ball flight from their wedge to their 7-iron, but complain how the ball flight starts to become unmanageable as the club gets longer, and how the ball flight is really bad with their driver. They think their swing is changing, but that's usually not the case. The reason the ball flight is dramatically different between their short clubs compared with their longer clubs is magnification. Shorter irons are swung with less speed than longer clubs, imparting much less sidespin and backspin than the longer ones. So, if you hit a 9-iron and a 4-iron with the identical face angle and clubhead path, the amount of curvature would be much greater with the 4-iron. End result is your longer clubs tell the tale, revealing bad swing mechanics. Get it looked at.

MASTER·STROKES

Intentional Fade

A shot that "fades" from left to right is sometimes very useful. It is great for all shots on holes that bend right or for a well-guarded pin position on the right side of the green.

Here's how to hit a fade:

1) Line up the leading edge of the clubface square to where you want the shot to finish.

2) Align feet, hips, knees and shoulders slightly open or left of your target line.

3) Swing normally along your body line. This should put a slight clockwise or fade spin on the ball.

4) If you find that your shots fly straight instead of fading, make one extra adjustment: Turn your hands a shade to the left on the grip. This encourages a slightly more open clubface at impact, and more fade.

DRAW, Partner!

The draw is a weapon all good golfers should have in their arsenal. A draw shot flies low and right-to-left. This shot helps fight the wind. It also takes advantage of firm fairways by running after landing. The ball comes off the face low and stays low. This is because you make contact with a slightly closed clubface, giving the ball counterclockwise spin.

Here's how to hit it:

1. Set up your body in a normal stance, aiming right of the target line.

2. Set up so that the ball is two to three inches farther back than normal in your stance. (Note: Make sure the club's leading edge is square to the target line. Be careful – there's a tendency to leave the clubface open or pointing right after you move the ball back.)

3. Make a grip adjustment by turning both hands slowly right on your handle,

away from the target.

4. Take a normal, free, full swing, making sure to release the club fully through impact. The results will be a strong, low, right-to-left draw shot.

SQUARE

Section 6:

MASTER·STROKES

Don't 'Get A Grip,' Get Your Grip

There is no perfect grip. The history of golf is loaded with great players who have held the club in different ways. Lee Trevino had a strong grip, hands turned to the right. Johnny Miller had a weak grip, hands turned to the left. But there are basics for a good grip to hit repetitive, solid shots:

1) The club should rest primarily in the fingers, rather than the palms.

2) The hands should be "knitted" together (overlap or interlock grip) so they work as a single unit.

3) Both hands should be positioned in a natural way that makes it easiest to return the clubface squarely to the target at impact.

The grip is the connection of the golfer to the golf club. If a golfer can return the clubface squarely to the golf ball with speed and consistency, he has found the perfect grip for himself. If you're not hitting straight, solid shots, you should experiment to find your "perfect grip."

SQUARE IMPACT

Swing Basics

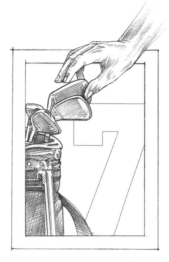

SECTION 7:
Short Irons

You hit a long drive down the middle of the fairway and are looking at an 8-iron approach shot over a deep sand trap. Now what? Well, ideally, a well-aimed, well-struck shot that flies up over the trap and nestles next to the pin. It's not that simple, of course. But it's not so difficult either—especially if you follow these tips.

CONTENTS

Solid Irons 101

If you're starting a new season or just taking up the game, you need to have the "basics" down for solid iron play. Without these basics, you will never hit consistently good iron shots. Here are the keys to a good setup and posture. 1. Align the clubface square to the target line, with feet, knees, hips and shoulders perfectly parallel to your target line. 2. Position the ball slightly ahead of center of your feet, with your hands set 1 to 2 inches ahead of ball. This sets you up to deliver a slightly descending blow that adds backspin and control. 3. Develop a balanced and athletic posture, with your arms hanging naturally rather than reaching, and with your weight between the balls and heels of your feet. This puts you in position to make a good turn without any extraneous movement and deliver the clubface squarely at impact.

First Things First

We see many golfers change their swings, their grips, their clubs – just about everything whenever they struggle. Remember this classic piece of advice from the great Jack Nicklaus: When you begin to struggle and solid ball contact is inconsistent, always look to your ball position first. This crucial fundamental, when incorrect, will affect your entire swing. Always be certain to check that your ball position for wedges and short irons is right in the center of your stance – longer irons and fairway woods a few inches more forward. The driver ball position should be off the inside of the heel of your front foot.

Short Irons

Tee Time

All players, especially seniors, should tee the ball up every chance they get. You'll see many players drop a ball in the tee box on par-3s and hit as if they were in the fairway. This isn't a good idea because you are giving away a decided advantage. On holes with a distance that requires you to select a 5-iron up to a 2-iron, you should tee the ball up 1/4 to 1/2 an inch. On shorter holes requiring a 6-iron or less up to a wedge, you should tee the ball up no more than 1/4 of an inch. Teeing the ball up always increases your ability to "get all of it" for maximum carry, allowing you to select a shorter club that is easier to hit.

You also eliminate the chance of grass getting between the clubface and ball at impact, causing the shot to fly and have less backspin upon landing.

Note: It's a great idea for seniors to tee up all practice shots while at the driving range. This will help reduce the amount of times their hands, arms and shoulders will suffer from the impact of smashing an iron clubhead into the turf. Your body and its joints will thank you by rewarding you with a long, injury-free season.

Section 7:

Lofty Goals

Amateurs usually underestimate the distance adjustment needed to reach the target for an approach shot from an uphill lie. They mistakenly think one club longer or swinging harder than normal will get the job done to reach the elevated green. What these amateurs don't realize is that an uphill lie adds a lot of loft at impact, shortening the shot more than they would think. Let's say you're playing from an upslope of 12 degrees. This means the ball will take off at an angle three clubs shorter than off a level lie (since the difference in loft between each club is about 4 degrees). So you need to assess the slope angle and adjust. If you are playing off an upslope as steep as 12 degrees, do the math, use an iron three clubs longer than normal then make your normal swing.

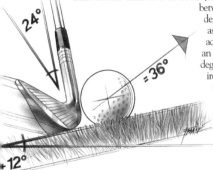

Short Irons

Slopes Throw A Nasty Curve

It's important to keep in mind, while playing a hilly course, how sidehill lies affect ball flight. It's a shame to hit the ball great and watch it go right or left because your head wasn't in the game.

If the ball is below your feet and you make perfectly square contact, the ball will fade or slice right. To adjust for this lie, bend your knees slightly more than usual to help get the clubhead down to the ball, choke up a bit (hands toward butt end of club) and aim for the left edge of the green. The ball will fade back to the middle.

If the ball is above your feet, it will draw or hook left if struck squarely. To adjust to this lie, choke down on the club (hands toward clubhead) to give you room for good contact, and aim for the right edge of the green. The ball will draw back to the middle. As on any draw shot, the ball will run longer.

Clip Your Irons

How many times have you been told to "hit down" on your iron shots, causing you to dig a substantial divot beyond impact? It hurts just thinking about it. As a senior, you need to realize that hitting down sharply puts great strain on the hands and wrists and can easily lead to an injury. Also, a steep descent increases the chances of hitting the shot "fat." To help avoid this swing path, visualize your downswing as more circular through the hitting zone rather than V-shaped. To help you clip your irons, position the ball between the center of your stance and a line opposite your left heel. You'll contact the ball with the clubhead just moving slightly downward to its lowest point, which is just past the ball. Clean, solid, injury-free shots will result.

Don't Be A Fat Head!

    You hit a nice drive, and your ball is lying in the middle of the fairway, awaiting a short iron shot to the green. You might be ramped up a bit, so you lunge for the ball, allowing your head and shoulders to move down on the downswing, and hit the ball "FAT." Hitting it fat means you struck the turf behind the ball first, slowing the club's momentum. The ball sadly bloops forward only a fraction of the distance to the target.

    This is one of the most maddening and embarrassing shots in golf, most often caused by a downward head movement. To stop the fat shot, you must keep your head in place. To help you do this, imagine that your head is in a box suspended in the air, keeping it from moving up or down (some lateral movement is OK). Then make your body turn away from and then back through the ball, while keeping your head and body level. You'll strike the ball with a slightly downward, nipping blow for a crisp iron shot instead of digging a grave for your score card.

STEADY HEAD

FAT HIT

CLEAN HIT

Shape Your Shots By Hand

Better golfers put sidespin on their iron shots to get the ball close to flags right or left. There's a simple method to help you do this: Align your body and the clubface to the middle of the green. To "draw" a shot toward a pin on the left, grip lightly with your left hand but more firmly with your right. This right-hand pressure encourages you to release or close the face through impact, imparting right-to-left draw spin. If the pin is tucked right, grip more firmly with the left hand and lightly with the right. You'll make contact with the clubface a shade open so that the ball flies with a touch of left-to-right "fade" spin toward the flag.

Short Irons

Old Reliable

Being a regular golfer, through the years you hopefully have acquired the ability to draw or fade the ball. If this is so, this can be a reliable answer to hit approach shots close in crosswinds – normally a very tricky situation.

Let's say the pin placement is on the left side of the green and the crosswind is howling left to right. We know a straight shot will be blown off the flag and roll more right after landing. The way to counter this problem would be to hit a draw. You want to hit this shot starting out just right of the hole with your draw spin on it. The counter left ball spin will help hold the shot's line in the crosswind. This ball will also land softly due to its curve fighting the wind. One last tip: Stepping up one club longer than normal will also help counter that crosswind.

You Gotta Know When To Back Off

Most of the time, we tell our students to make sure they get the ball to the hole on their approach shots to the green. This is because they usually underclub. They try to kill their iron and, more often than not, end up well short of the hole. There are situations when short of the hole is strategically exactly where you want to be. For example, you want to underclub when the pin is placed at the back of a green that slopes downhill from back to front. It's very difficult to get up and down from behind greens in a situation like this. Down is BAD. You have way better odds with an uphill putt. Even an uphill chip is an easier shot. Don't just hit, THINK!

Short Irons

Good Choking

Here's a great little trick to help out when accuracy is more important than distance. Simply "choke down" on the club slightly. This adjustment is most effective on short- to midiron shots (pitching wedge through 5-iron) where you have an opening to the flag. If there are no hazards between you and the pin, you don't have to hit the ball extra high. This is an especially good idea if the wind is blowing.

Take one club more than normal – for example, an 8-iron rather than a 9-iron. Choke up by moving your hands 1 inch up the grip away from the butt end. Then take your normal swing, making sure to swing "within yourself," maintaining good balance. This small adjustment increases your chances of making good, solid contact much higher. This will produce a lower ball flight than normal, but a highly accurate shot that holds its line to the flag, maybe hitting it stiff.

MASTER·STROKES

Punch The Wind

As the season continues through the fall, you will find yourself hitting "approach shots" into strong winds. In these conditions, use the "punch shot." This is a low-trajectory shot you can keep under stronger winds, giving you more control. It has less spin and more roll.

Here's an example: If you're a wedge away in normal, calm weather, use a 7-iron. Grip down on the shaft 2 inches. Position the ball in the middle of your stance, slightly farther back than normal. Make a 3/4 backswing, then hit down crisply, transferring your weight aggressively to the front foot. Follow through with your club pointing toward the target, keeping the lead wrist firm and flat. It should feel as though you're hitting an extra-long chip shot. The ball will take off low and straight, boring through the wind rather than getting caught up in it.

choke down

Short Irons

MASTER·STROKES

Different Strokes For Different Pokes

Not all swings share the same follow-through. The speed generated by fully swinging a long-shafted driver has the club **short vs** ending up hanging down your **long** back or resting on your neck (check out John Daly). However, when swinging your 9-iron, the follow-through will be shorter and more controlled. Your swing might end up with the club and your hands in the air in front of you (check out Phil Mickelson). It's kind of like a big jet needing a longer runway to land than a single-engine prop plane does. Ripping a driver requires an all-out full finish, while your short irons are meant to be played with finesse, with a compact, more controlled finish.

Be A Man!

Hey, macho man, be a real man and don't let your ego get in the way of hitting a nice, smooth wedge shot. Too many amateurs, especially the guys, are influenced by watching how far the pros can hit approach shots. A touring pro will typically hit a pitching wedge 135 yards and a sand wedge 115. If you can hit the green with those clubs from those distances, it's probably an "all-out swing." Swinging out of your shoes will result in a loss of accuracy.

A better approach is never swinging with more than 85 percent effort with your 8- and 9-irons or your pitching and sand wedges. Remember to choose the club that will allow you to swing at 85 percent, meaning swing easy with more club. You'll find yourself hitting it stiff and consistently close to the flag.

Short Irons

MASTER·STROKES

Master The Tweeners

We have all found ourselves at that certain yardage that is right in between clubs. Let's say it's too long for a 9-iron, but too short for an 8-iron. Here is a sure way to be confident and make more birdies from the in-between distance. Take the longer club and simply choke down an inch on the grip. Then make your normal golf swing. You will find that gripping down an inch on the handle will take off a little bit of your normal distance but enhances control. This extra control will make it very easy to hit the shot solidly and accurately. Avoid taking the shorter club and trying to kill it. This is a sure way to hit an unsolid, wild shot and ruin the hole.

Divot Detective

Divots are a great form of feedback because they tell you a lot about your clubhead path relative to your target. For example, if you see the divot pointing straight to the left, the club is swinging from outside in. Players who

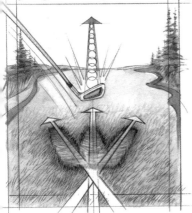

swing from outside in tend to have a relatively steep angle of approach, which creates divots that tend to be deeper, larger and point to the left. Players who swing too much from the inside tend to have a shallower angle of approach and take shallower divots that point to the right.

Short Irons

SECTION 8:
Pitching

The wedge shot ranks as one of the most commonly misunderstood and mishit. Yet we all know that guy who can step up to a wedge or half-wedge or quarter-wedge shot and stick it close almost every time. Here's how you can become that guy.

CONTENTS

Which Pitch?

High-lofted pitch shots are pretty, but they are not always the right pitch. Unless you're extremely adept with a very lofted wedge, they can be tricky to hit perfectly, and they do need to be hit perfectly. These shots require a lot of finesse. Without having great touch, being able to dial in pinpoint, exact distance or stop it dead and spin it back is not likely to happen. Too many things can go wrong – you usually underhit it, with the ball going nowhere, or you kill it, sending the ball flying over the green into trouble.

So, until you're ready, a lower-flying pitch that will land sooner, then run to the hole is a better choice because it is a lot more controllable. Whenever there is a clear path to the pin without any hazards, you want to take advantage and hit a more predictable, higher-odds pitch and run, giving you better control for more accuracy and leaving you a short "one-putt."

SAFER SHOT

How Do I Stand?

One of the most important fundamentals in golf is posture. It becomes especially important as we age. Golfers tend to get in better posture while hitting full-swing shots, but as the shots get closer the posture slouches. Remember that you bow from the hips, not the waist. Keep that back nice and straight with the shoulders over the feet. This is the same posture for chipping, pitching and sand as well as putting.

If the posture slouches, then the framework of the swing cannot be supported. This simply means the body cannot pivot or move freely, resulting in a slapping or scooping motion with the hands.

BEND
FROM
HIP

Don't Leave Yourself Short

Here's an incredible stat: 80 percent of all amateurs hit their approach shots short.

Instead of sitting on the green looking at a par, the "underclubbing" left their approach shot short and off the green. Now they have to "chip up," or worse, they're sitting in a bunker or are wet.

Here's a tip to be "pin-high." Assume the pin is at the middle depth on the green, and any trouble is equal, front or back. Select the club that, if you hit it perfectly, the ball would reach the back fringe of the green. Yep! Let your "perfect" hits be a little long. The simple truth is that you will hit the majority of your shots a little less than perfect, maybe 80 percent. The end result is that by "overclubbing," you'll hit most of your approach shots pin-high. An extra benefit is that your poorly hit shots will reach the front of the green rather than being way short.

Being Square Makes You Go Straight

What's the good of making a beautiful swing and solid contact only to look up and watch your ball land off to the side of the green or in a hazard because you didn't line up your club squarely? Too many amateur golfers are guilty of this, particularly with the shorter irons. This is because they get fooled -- they tend to look at the more rounded top line of the clubhead when they address the ball.

Instead, carefully focus on aligning the straight leading edge of the clubface to your target as you set up. Imagine a square lying on the ground at a perfect right angle to your target line, and make sure your scoring lines are parallel to that square. On-line approach shots will follow.

MASTER·STROKES

Ball Placement For The Short Shots

Ball placement can be confusing for a lot of golfers especially when it comes to the short game shots. For example a thirty-yard pitch shot that requires loft on the shot, the ball position is critical. I use this little phrase to help everyone determine where the ball should go. Left for loft which means toward the forward foot and right for roll for the back foot. The more forward in the stance the higher the ball will go and vice-versa.

LOWER   HIGHER

MASTER·STROKES

Extra Loft From Downhill Lie

Approach shots from downhill lies are tough for all players, especially for seniors who often have trouble lofting their shots. Let's say you have a severe 12-degree downhill lie. Remember, you must take a shorter club, with more loft than the distance would call for from a level lie. If you are a 7-iron distance from the green on a steep downslope, use no more than a P-wedge. Swing down and through the shot rather than trying to lift it. Because of the downslope you're on, the wedge face will move through impact with the loft of no more than a 7-iron. Always remember that when in doubt from downhill lies, take the more-lofted club.

48°-12°=36°

Knee High Bend

Many courses will leave you with an uphill or downhill lie on your approach shot. Of course, these situations can make your shot tricky, because you could easily lose your balance. You will certainly mishit the ball if you're falling backward or forward during your swing. A simple adjustment to help steady your body is to bend your "uphill knee." By bending, we mean significantly more bend than your downhill knee. Bending the knee that is uphill will help compensate for the steep slope. This will keep your upper-body weight on a more vertical line, as opposed to leaning too much down the slope. This uphill-knee bend will give you the best balance possible during your swing. One more piece of advice: Take plenty of club so you can make an extra-smooth swing.

BEND
UPHILL
KNEE

MASTER·STROKES

3-Point Range

Most amateur players make the same mistake over and over again. They constantly leave their approach shots short of pin high. Many of these short shots often roll back off the green. I advise my students to actually try to land their approach shots on top of the flagstick. Make believe you're trying to drain that 3-pointer at the buzzer – you know, that focused, "in the zone" feeling. By aiming for the top of the flagstick, suddenly the player finds his ball pin high or a bit long, rather than short of the green over and over again. If a player doesn't make perfect contact, he still has enough distance to get the ball up onto the putting surface.

Pitching

Better Pitching

At impact, many recreational golfers wind up with the shaft leaning away from the target and a collapsed left wrist. This position leads to fat and thin shots, as well as inconsistent distance control. To hit crisp pitches, at impact the shaft must be leaning slightly toward the target.

You can achieve this by positioning the ball in the center of your stance, distributing your weight toward your left leg for a right-handed player (and inversely, right leg for a left-handed player), then making a swing focusing on hitting the ball first and then brushing the turf just in front of the ball.

Pin Spin

There are situations in which you need to stop your ball quickly after it lands on the green. For example, a tight pin placement with sand or water between you and the pin, and you're trying to save par. Or a severe downslope or hazard just past the hole. To stop your ball where you want, you will need to be able to put backspin on your wedge shot. Here's a backspin trick. When hitting short pitch or wedge shots, imagine that your wedge is a knife, and on the downswing you want to slice off a fraction of the back of the ball with the blade's leading edge. This image will help you make the sharp descending blow that produces maximum backspin.

Use this slicing motion only on "less-than-full-swing" wedge shots, not full swings with the longer irons. Also, a soft-covered ball makes it much easier to put backspin "STOP" on these shots.

Cut a Slice

Pitching

MASTER·STROKES

The Right Approach

When you are faced with a short 20-yard shot and not a lot of green to work with, club selection is very important. The mistake a lot of golfers make is using a less-lofted club like a 9-iron or pitching wedge. This is often very hard to control the distance. I recommend a 60-degree wedge, which has more loft and will give you a higher and softer shot. You make the same swing as a chip stroke, so no need to try anything fancy – the club does it for you. Practice using sand wedges around the green – they're not just for the sand.

Use Your Knees

When playing the short pitch from light rough, use your right knee as a focal point. Ken Venturi, one of my greatest mentors, has taught players such as Tom Watson, Tom Weiskopf and John Cook to use the right knee as an accelerator. You time your hands and your right knee to develop a consistent feel for any short pitch shot.

Just Imagine You're At The Beach

You missed the green. Fear strikes when you arrive at your ball to find you're lying nice in the grass, but there is a hazard between your ball and a tight pin. Why don't you feel this uptight when you're in a greenside bunker? Because you have learned a dependable procedure that you follow that confidently gets you up and down from the sand.

Relax, the same procedure works just as well to hit that delicate lob shot.

FIRST, open the face of your lob or sand wedge. **SECOND,** play the ball slightly ahead of center in your stance. **THIRD,** keep your weight on your front foot. **FOURTH,** hit an inch or two behind the ball. Remember to finish high, just like you do from a bunker shot. There it is, a simple 1-2-3-4 way to lob it close.

Lob Lie Logic

Golf courses that have a lot of mounding around the greens will have you facing recovery shots that call for a high, soft lob shot to get the ball close to the hole. Before you decide to play this type of delicate shot, you must remember to check your lie closely. In order to play a soft lob successfully, you must be able to slip the clubface of your most lofted club under the ball, rather than hitting down on it. Therefore, you must have a good cushion of grass between the bottom of the ball and the turf. If the ball is lying "tight" to the ground, the degree of precision needed to strike the shot correctly is so high that playing the lob is not worth the risk. A "skulled" or "blooped" shot could lead to a disastrous hole. So, you need to make sure the ball is sitting "up" before committing to the lob shot.

TOO TIGHT   SITTING "UP"

Soft + Slow = Success

You know you're not Phil Mickelson, but you are in the same situation you saw hi[m] in on TV last weekend. You have a greenside bunker between you and a close pin plac[e]ment. What's needed is a "Phil-type" high, soft lob shot that will stop quickly. Much [of] the secret in this type of shot is in the swing tempo. Select your most-lofted club. Set u[p] with the ball placed forward in your stance, so your hands are even or slightly behind th[e] ball at address. Make a long and very, very slow backswing. Then swing the club dow[n] just as slowly as you brought it back. You should feel that your swing is taking longer than necessary, almost as if it's underwater. This extreme slow tempo causes the clubhead to come through the ball on a very shallow arc, giving you maximum loft on the clubface at impact and producing a high, soft-landing shot that will quickly stop. Now practice your distances for this shot so you have it in your arsenal.

Weak Is Better
For Soft Lob Shot

Many casual players have developed a wonderful grip for full-swing long shots. They have learned that a strong grip with the "V's" formed between their thumbs and forefingers pointing to their back shoulder will assist them in adding distance by launching the ball lower and longer, with a draw spin. However, they keep this same grip when they need to hit the high lob shot over a bunker from 40 to 50 yards. This grip hurts their ability to hit a high, soft and accurate shot to the pin. This grip will tend to result in a lower, left-moving shot. Remember, you need to weaken your grip for these soft-landing pitches. Adjust your V's, rotating them toward your left until they point more to your nose.

275   **Pitching**

MASTER·STROKES

Palm Under For Lob Shots

You're looking at a tight pin placement with a nasty hazard in between you and the flag. You need to hit a very high, soft lob shot that will get over the hazard and stop after landing. You are trying to stop the ball with trajectory, not spin. To do this, the clubface has to remain open throughout the swing. Open your stance and aim left. Weaken your grip by rotating your hands to the left, and open the clubface. Your right palm and hand should be under and behind your left hand at and well after impact. Fight the urge to roll your wrist or close the face through the hitting zone. This is a high-risk, high-reward shot. Try this shot from a good lie – a little cushion but not too much.

Lobbying For Safety

The pin is very close to the edge of the green. You're left with a short pitch from tangled rough. There is a bunker between you and the hole. You must pop the ball up high and soft, and stop it quick to get it close. No easy task, unless you're Phil Mickelson. It's a very risky shot that requires a lot of touch. This is even more difficult for golfers whose finesse and technique might not be as razor-sharp as you'd prefer. It would most likely be bad strategy to try to execute that perfect shot. A better strategy would be to plan a safe recovery. Select a landing spot well over the bunker, maybe with an uphill putt. Swing your sand or lob wedge with enough force to get it there. Let the ball release and run past the hole as opposed to trying to "flop" the ball dead. It's OK if you leave yourself a 20-footer. You might make it, but you'll know you played a smart shot.

Pitch & Run

Don't leave home without the long-pitch-and-run shot in your bag. From 75 yards on in, it's a better choice than the lofted shot. You don't have to worry about the ball being held up by a head wind, misdirected by a crosswind or overshot with the wind at your back. The beauty is landing the ball short of the green, then letting it skip and "check" on the green.

Select a 7- or 8-iron, and set up with a slightly narrow, open stance. Keep your shoulders parallel to this position, with 60 percent of your weight on your front foot. Play the ball back slightly and stand erect. Lean the shaft forward toward the target, putting your hands slightly ahead of the ball. Grip down only an inch, with the clubface square to slightly open, depending on the height and spin required.

Swing back no higher than shoulder level, being sure to let your wrists cock. On the downswing, push your front knee toward the target, letting your arms and weight shift effortlessly and direct your club back to the ball. It's paramount that you let the right hand rotate over the left through impact.

Don't Leave Your Mark!

Those beautifully struck short-iron shots that land on the green from high above usually leave a ball mark. It's your responsibility to find your mark and make the repair. We all benefit from this good etiquette.

1

To repair a ball mark, use either a ball-mark repair tool or a golf tee. Use the prongs to lift the indented part of the ball-mark area (the dimple created by the force of the ball) slightly up. Then use the prongs to pull back the small flap of the turf at the other side of the mark (the outer edge of the crater). Don't try to lift up this side.

2

Finally, pat the area flat to the putting surface with the bottom sole of your putter.

SECTION 9:
Chipping

Chipping a ball those last few feet onto the green and letting it roll up next to the hole looks so easy. It is, actually, easy. You just need to practice and apply these tips.

CONTENTS

MASTER·STROKES

Chipping 101

The chip shot is for when your ball is lying just off the green. ADVICE: If the ground between your ball and the green is smooth, putt! Your worst putt is usually better than your worst chip. The rule in chipping is "minimum air time, maximum ground time." The chip is just a long putt with modifications. Use your putting grip with a firm left wrist and 70 percent of your weight on your left side. Your stance should be narrow, with the ball back and close to your body. Hands should be slightly ahead of the ball at address to encourage a slight descending hit, and they should stay ahead throughout the stroke. Take the club up slightly on the backswing with a little wrist hinge, and make a slight downward brush coming through, with the left wrist remaining solid through the shot. Use a 7-iron for long chips, with the ball traveling 1/4 in the air and rolling 3/4 on ground. For shorter chips, use an 8-iron with a ratio of 1/3 air to 2/3 ground. If you have only a little green to work with or you need more loft, use a pitching wedge and a 50/50 air/ground ratio.

FIRM-WRISTED STROKE

MASTER·STROKES

Use An Arsenal To WIN At Chipping

Avoid falling in love with just one club and using it for all of your chip shots. It's fine and dandy to have a favorite. However, it helps to have an arsenal of clubs for all of the different chipping situations you will face. For example, a long chip shot with lots of green to run the ball across might be better suited for a less-lofted, flatter-faced 7- or 8-iron than, say, a very lofted lob or sand wedge. Good players use the same chipping stroke, but switch the club to negotiate different distances.

SAND, LOB WEDGE OR 7-8 IRON

Chipping

MASTER·STROKES

Chipping, The Great Par Saver!

If you want to save par, you MUST be able to chip from just off the green. Using the loft of a short iron like a 7-, 8- or 9-iron, you want to carry the ball several feet onto the green so that it can land clean and run to the hole like a putt.

The key to good chipping is (1) keeping your wrist firm and (2) having your hands leading the club through impact. You need to choke down on the grip (almost touching the shaft) and execute the stroke with a movement of your arms and shoulders. Place the ball back in your stance, then make your stroke with a slightly downward blow rather than scooping at the ball. By using an arm-and-shoulder chipping stroke and keeping your hands ahead through impact, you make precise contact. This helps avoid scuffing the ground, which results in leaving the chip way short.

True Lies

A short chip from off the green should be lofted just onto the green so it can roll to the hole after landing. This is because you want a clean, true roll for accuracy on a nice, smooth putting surface. You want to avoid bouncing the ball into irregular, less-predictable grass just off the green. To accomplish this, you must select the proper lofted club. You will need to know how the lie will affect the shot.

For example, let's say your ball is 8 feet off the green and 40 feet from the pin, lying on nice fairway grass. An 8-iron should give you the right lift and roll.

If your shot is the same exact distance away but your ball is lying in snarly rough, remember that the ball will come out lower, with less backspin. You will need to compensate by using a more lofted club like a pitching wedge or a sand wedge. So read your lie before you chip, then choose your weapon.

Chipping

MASTER·STROKES

Be Consistently Up 'N' Down

Usually "up 'n' down" would mean being inconsistent. In the game of golf, that's a good thing. It means chipping the ball from off the green up onto the green, then a "one-putt" down into the hole to save par. To score your best, you must be able to do this consistently whenever your approach shot finishes a little off the putting surface.

To become good at green-side chips, you must practice. Here's a chipping game to keep it fun.

Drop three balls alongside the practice green. Chip them at the pin. Move to the other side of the green and repeat. Keep moving, but you can't leave until you hole at least one. As you improve, change your goal to sinking two, then three. Remember, you can't leave until you've met your goal. This dedicated practice will sharpen your feel, and most of your chips will finish very close. You will elevate your game and lower your scores.

MASTER·STROKES

Dress Rehearsal Helps You Brush Up!

Many poor chippers of the golf ball fail to realize that to be successful at routine green-side chip shots, it is vital to make a downward, or descending, stroke. You cannot lift or scoop the ball up in the air. When we instruct our students in chipping, we always have them learn a pre-chip-shot routine that includes two or three practice strokes where they brush the grass in their downstroke. These "rehearsal" strokes will teach the proper downward stroke. This also creates a nice rhythmic feel, making it much easier to repeat when it's time to chip the ball.

Hit Down

once

twice

then Hit

MASTER·STROKES

One-Armed-Bandit Chipper

Many casual golfers "break down" on their chip shots. That is, the left wrist flips or scoops at the ball. Here's a great drill to help this problem. Take the club in your left hand only. Place the ball in the center or toward the back of your stance (delofting the club). Place 60 percent of your weight on the front foot. Lean the shaft forward at address. Position your head in front of the ball. Backswing and follow-through should be equal distances. Keep your lower body still on the backswing, with very little leg action as well on the forward swing.

At impact, keep your left arm and club in a straight line. Your left wrist is to remain flat and firm. With left-arm-only practice, struggling chippers will get the correct feel.

NO

LEAD WRIST FIRM

FRANK

Uphill Chips

The amateur golfer invariably will face a chip from an uphill lie. This scenario usually winds up with the amateur coming up short, leaving him a "knee-knocking" putt for par. This is because the amateur makes a "mental" error, overlooking that you will not get your usual chipping distance from an uphill lie on account of hitting into sloping terrain.

My simple but highly successful recommendation is to imagine a small bull's-eye target 5 to 10 feet beyond the flagstick. Then try to chip your ball to this imaginary spot. Your effort to run the ball farther will be counterbalanced by the uphill resistance you will encounter into the slope. The end result will leave your ball around the flag. Of course, with practice, you will get a better "feel" for this shot. This simple "mental game" trick will work almost every time.

MASTER·STROKES

A Clean Sweep

A great drill for better chipping is using a broom. Take the broom and make a few short chip strokes as if you were sweeping up debris. When you sweep you actually keep the handle of the broom leading the face of the broom. A chip stroke is the same. The handle leads the clubface to impact and lifts the ball up in the air. If at any time the clubhead passes the handle, the results are very poor. By using this drill you get the correct feel to help you with chipping and a better understanding of the proper technique.

Sweep

MASTER·STROKES

Lob Wedge When The Rough Gets Going

The basic chip shot is a low-running shot from just off the green. The idea is to roll your ball a greater distance than it flies. You want to loft your ball just enough so that it lands on the green by about 3 feet, then begins to roll. The reason is that this is a much more predictable – and therefore more controllable – shot. It avoids irregularities in longer grass, along with bare spots. A chip shot also uses a smaller, more controlled motion.

But if your ball is lying in deep, snarly rough, remember that the ball will come out lower and with less backspin. You'll need to play this chip with a more lofted club like your lob wedge to ensure you clear the rough and land your ball on the putting surface. Remember, the shorter and more lofted the iron, the higher the shot and shorter the roll. Conversely, the longer the iron, the lower the flight and longer the roll. This is why you need to reach for your lob wedge when the going gets rough.

LOWER FLIGHT

MORE ROLL

Chipping

Chip Tight Lie Into Slopes

You're looking at an uphill chip because you've overshot the green. The flag is close to your side, not leaving you any room to stop the ball. At first, you're thinking a high, soft lob shot will do the trick. However, as you walk up to your ball, you discover your lie is tight, with no cushion under the ball, making a lob shot too risky. Your high-percentage shot is a low chip into the slope ahead of you. Select a club (usually a 5-, 6- or 7-iron) that, used with your normal chip setup and swing, will carry the ball halfway up the bank with enough speed to climb the rest of the way up and onto the green. This chip shot into the slope is definitely a "feel shot" – practice it so you will have it when you need it.

MASTER·STROKES

Texas Style

Chips from firm ground or hardpan call for precise contact, compared with a chip from soft fairway turf. When there is no cushion under the ball, it's very easy to hit behind it and leave it way short. This is even more likely when playing a lofted chip.

So if you have a lie on hard, dry, fairly level ground around the green, your putter, also known as a "Texas wedge," is your best choice.

You can reasonably use the putter up to 20 yards off the green. Just read the speed and the break of the shot as you would a long putt, for that's really what it is. You will see that chips played with your Texas wedge will finish much closer to the hole on average.

Chipping

Wood Chips

Here's a great little tip for those golfers who have trouble with their "touch" and club selection on delicate short chips just off the green. Use a 5-wood instead of one of your short irons. This works well when your ball is barely into the light rough, where you can't use a putter because the ball may hop out erratically. Simply use your normal putting stroke, but replace your putter with the more lofted fairway 5-wood. Open your stance and choke down a little on the club shaft.

The loft on the face helps get the ball up and out of the light rough, then lands it onto the fringe, rolling nice and smoothly. Practice this shot and you'll be rewarded by consistently rolling your chips close to the hole.

SECTION 10:
Sand Traps

Sand traps may be officially designated as hazards. But there's no reason they should be hazardous to your handicap. As you'll see in the tips that follow, hitting out of a greenside trap under normal circumstances is actually one of the easiest shots in golf. But that doesn't mean the circumstances will always be normal, or that the trap you land in will always be right next to the green. Fear not. With these tips, you can learn to hit almost any sand shot with confidence and satisfying results.

CONTENTS

Bunker Basics

Bottoming Out The key to successful sand play is to use the bottom, sole or flange (all the same thing) of the sand wedge, not the leading edge. The wedge has "bounce" built into the design of the sole, meaning the back edge of the club is lower than the front edge. This bounce, used correctly, allows the club to skid through the sand (not dig in) under the ball and lift it out of the sand. The club doesn't contact the ball – a cushion of sand carries the ball out. Take a slightly open stance, your weight a little on your left side (60 percent). Work your feet into the sand, anchoring them. Position the ball slightly forward of center. Open the clubface, take a lazy swing (making a minimum weight shift on the backswing) and let the club travel up with a free cocking of the wrist. Make a good shoulder turn with a long, relaxed swing. Get the club down and through the ball, slapping the sand 3 to 4 inches behind the ball as you turn through, and finish facing the target.

Hit 3" to 4" BEHIND BALL

OPEN STANCE

BALL FORWARD

Be The Sand Man

Many golfers panic when they come upon their ball in a greenside bunker. This fear could be overcome if they only would commit to the practice needed to slay this dragon. The greenside-bunker shot is really very easy. You need to dedicate one hour a week in the sand. Golfers would lower their scores dramatically if they could improve their bunker play. For a good lie, the basics are to set up with an open stance and an open leading edge. Dig your feet in. Play the ball a little forward and hit 2$^{1/2}$ inches behind the ball. Swing square along your body line (outside-in to target line). Take a bigger swing than you think is necessary. Make a full weight shift. There are many other sand situations, so keep an eye on this feature for more sand tips.

ONE WEEK

Slow But Sure

Some tips that can improve your game are so simple. Here's one from the great Jack Nicklaus. He has stated that he got his best results out of greenside bunkers if he swung in "slow motion." That is, follow the textbook. Dig your feet in, open your stance, open the leading edge and play the ball as a normal fairway iron or slightly more forward. Take a bigger swing than normal, swinging squarely along your body line and hitting the sand 2 1/2 inches behind the ball. BUT DO IT SLOWLY, as if you were moving in slow motion, like instant replay. This nice, calm, deliberate motion will have you out of the sand and on the green every time for your "up and down."

Sand Smart

Being aware of sand conditions is important when playing a green-side bunker. You cannot use the same setup and approach on all sand shots.

Whether the sand is deep versus shallow should dictate how you set up to play a successful shot. As you wiggle your feet into the sand to address the ball, you should be able to gauge the depth of the sand.

Shallow sand tends to be hard, which can cause your clubhead to bounce off the surface behind the ball so you "skull" the shot, sending the ball across the green. So when you're in hard sand, you need to square the face of your sand wedge so that the leading edge will dig in enough to get under the ball. Conversely, if you're in deeper sand that tends to be soft and fluffy, you want the clubhead to slide under rather than dig. To do this, you must open the blade wide. This exposes the trailing lower edge of the sand wedge flange so it will act like a rudder, causing the club to skim just under the surface and not allowing it to go deep, which would "flub" the shot and leave the ball in the bunker.

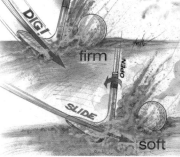

Adjust Follow-Through For Precision Sand Shots

Due to where your ball is located in a bunker, along with flag placement, you will always have the need to hit green-side bunker shots of different lengths.

To do this, you use the same basic swing, but you need to adjust the length of your follow-through, which alters the force of the swing to help vary the length of the shot.

To hit a short bunker shot (under 40 feet), make a full backswing, but instead of releasing the club like a normal sand shot, make it a short finish and hang on to it or block it – hold the face open as you finish. That makes the ball go shorter and land softly. Your hands should finish just below your waist. Don't take a little-bitty backswing and hit through the shot, because that greatly increases the chances of skulling the ball or leaving it in the bunker.

To hit a medium bunker shot (40 to 60 feet), make a full backswing and release the club normally through impact. Let your hands reach chest height, but don't go above your shoulders.

To hit a long bunker shot (over 60 feet), square the face, position the ball a little forward in your stance, then swing almost as if you're hitting a 3-wood. After a full backswing, accelerate through impact and all the way up to a full, high, long finish, with your hands above your shoulders.

I've worked very hard on bunker shots with tour pros like Tom Kite, Brad Faxon, Christie Kerr and Len Mattiace. This method produces great results.

Sand Traps

Be A Tiger For The Slot Bunker Blast

Many instructors advocate swinging outside-to-inside to hit a long bunker blast. Most amateurs tend to overdo this "cut" swing and lack the needed swing speed necessary to hit a longer bunker shot. Tiger Woods, as taught by Butch Harmon, loops the clubhead to the inside as he starts his downswing to blast the ball out of the sand. Watch Tiger on TV and take notes. Address the ball with a slightly open stance.

Play the ball just forward of center, and position the hands so the shaft doesn't lean toward the target. This keeps loft on the club and promotes an open clubface. Hinge the club early, getting the clubhead above your hands as soon as possible. As you set the club, turn your shoulders back. At the top, make a slight loop to the inside (lower the clubhead to a slightly "flatter" plane), dropping your club, hands and arms into the "slot." Release the clubhead earlier than normal. As you reach the hitting zone, continue to release early, contacting the sand 3 to 4 inches behind the ball. Pound that bunker with the flange of your sand wedge and continue through to your full finish.

Uphill Sand Shot

Your approach shot just came to rest on the upslope of a green-side bunker. This shot is trickier than your normal sand shot. You can easily pop the ball up and leave it well short. Or you can skull the ball, line-driving it over the green. But an uphill bunker shot is easier than a downhill bunker shot.

Here's how to play this shot successfully:

1. Set your feet securely, with weight evenly balanced and your shoulders parallel to the sand's slope. (This keeps you from digging in too deep.)

2. Position the ball no farther forward in your stance than opposite the inside of your left heel.

3. Aim to hit the sand a fraction closer to the ball than normal – say, 2 inches behind instead of 2 1/2 inches.

4. Swing normally.

If you judge that you can't fly the ball to the hole using a sand wedge, use a gap or pitching wedge instead.

gap wedge

2"

Sand Traps

Flat Trap, Flat Stick

Flat sand traps can be an opportunity for strategic golfers to get back some lost strokes on their score cards. If a sand trap is fairly flat, has a low lip and the lie is good, there is potential to putt out. Keeping the ball on the ground by putting the ball is more controllable, therefore leading to more predictable and accurate results. Let's say the lip of the trap is 15 feet away, the edge of the green 25 feet away and the flagstick 60 feet away. Try to imagine how much force you would need to putt the ball 60 feet, then add 50 percent more force to that stroke, because more energy will be needed to start the ball through the sand and the green-side fringe. Keep your stroke long, slow and level, and your head still. With this approach, you'll putt the ball out every time and, with practice, very often get it to finish close.

Bounce Yourself Out Of Traps

Having a hard time getting out of green-side bunkers? Some amateur or senior players don't realize that all sand wedges are not the same. If you are struggling in the sand, it's possible you're digging in too deep behind and under the ball. Looking at your ball still sitting in the trap after your shot is one of the most frustrating parts of the game.

Check the bottom of your sand wedge to see what "bounce angle" it has. This is the degree to which the rear edge of the club's sole is lower than the leading edge. The greater the bounce angle, the more the club will glide along just below the sand's surface, as opposed to digging in too deep. A sand wedge with a bounce angle of at least 12 degrees is a good choice. Twelve degrees will keep your clubhead moving through the sand even if it is very soft.

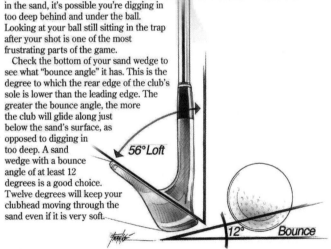

56° Loft

12° Bounce

Sand Traps

MASTER·STROKES

Buried Lie

There will be times you'll find your ball buried deeply in the face of a bunker. It might look like there's no way to get it out in one shot. It would take too much brute force, and you're not as young as you used to be. Here are two tips to help you escape more easily than you'd think in one shot. 1) Use a pitching wedge instead of a sand wedge. The sharper leading edge will cut into the sand and get under the ball better. 2) Address the ball with a square clubface as opposed to the open clubface you'd use from a good lie in the sand. This, too, helps the club dig deeper.

Hit down sharply 1 1/2 inches behind the ball, and don't worry about a follow-through. You'll be surprised at how easily the ball pops out.

Get Chippy In Bunkers

Here's a wise approach to the tough, long green-side bunker shot (25 to 50 yards).

This shot is especially difficult for casual players because it requires a lot of force to "blast" the ball out and all the way to the hole. Consider chipping your ball out if conditions permit. You need a good, clean lie in a bunker with a fairly low lip. Select an 8-iron, a 9-iron or a pitching wedge (lower loft for more run, more loft for less run). Take a narrow stance, choke well down on the grip for better control and position the ball back of center in your stance. Then swing with your arms, keeping your head and body still. Concentrate on hitting the ball first (unlike a normal bunker shot). The ball will come out low, then skip and roll all the way to the flag. The "bunker chip" can be a great weapon with practice.

choke down

ball back of center

Sand Traps

Sand Nip

We often see tremendous blasts of sand come up out of a green-side bunker when watching the pros. Many golfers believe that's always what's needed. The fact is, when a clubhead hits the sand far behind the ball and digs too deeply, it requires tremendous strength to keep the clubhead moving so the ball gets out. Amateurs should be thinking "nip" rather than "blast" from green-side bunkers. Assuming the lie is good, keep the clubface open and then simply try to nip a very shallow cut of sand out from under the ball. The less sand you can take, the less force you'll need. With practice, you'll find you can get the ball out and up on the green with much less strain.

1½"

½" TO ¾" DEEP

Pitching Wedge For Long Bunker Shot

For the strongest of golfers, bunker shots from 30 to 50 feet with a sand wedge are easy. This is not the case for some golfers who might have a little less strength. If your long sand wedge shots are coming up short, switch to your pitching wedge. Hitting with less loft will add distance. Make these minor adjustments: Aim more "square" to the target, and dig your feet in just slightly – if you dig in too deeply, you'll hit too far behind the ball. Try to contact the sand a bit closer to the ball than a greenside shot, say 2 inches instead of 2 ½ inches. Swing normally, and make sure to follow through fully. You'll be "up & down" again.

Note: For extreme cases, you might consider using a 9-iron.

SW   PW

Be Picky From Fairway Bunkers

The fairway bunker shot is one of the tougher shots in golf. It is crucial to realize how important it is to hit the ball first, NOT THE SAND first, in this situation. A thin-type shot is much better than a fat shot here. Take one extra club and grip down an inch, stand tall and stay very balanced. We teach our students to imagine that there is a pane of glass beneath their ball. Their goal is to pick the ball off the glass without breaking it. This image can help a lot with avoiding hitting too much sand.

CLUB UP

CHOKE DOWN

Take The Layup

Smart golfers and wise seniors will choose to "lay up" short of hazards as opposed to trying to hit the perfect long carry. You'll actually shoot lower scores with this approach. It sets you up, giving you the easiest possible shot to the pin. The aggressive approach requiring perfection will usually make you pay. Let's say you're laying up short of an elevated green guarded by a deep bunker. The green sits on a diagonal to the fairway with the pin at the right rear, a difficult placement. Do the following: 1) Aim for the left side of the fairway. This leaves you a diagonal shot angle, giving you more green to hit short of the flag. 2) Lay up well short so your next shot is 70-85 yards rather than 40-50. This way, you can hit a fuller shot with your sand wedge to put maximum backspin on the ball.

←EASIER SHOT TO HOLE

SECTION 11:
Problem Shots

Even the best-planned—and, sometimes, even the best hit—golf shot can end up in the deep rough, shallow water, a divot hole or another problem situation. But you can overcome these challenges by planning and hitting a good next shot. These tips will help.

CONTENTS

Rough Bunker

Your approach shot landed off to the side of the green where the pin is located, but it's sitting in some pretty tall green-side rough. Because the pin is so close, you do not have much room to stop the shot. Here's a trick to help you get up and down for your par. Play the shot like it's a green-side bunker shot. Address the ball with your sand wedge open or "laid back." Aim to hit a spot a full 2 inches behind the ball. Create a steep arc by cocking your wrist quickly. Hit down to your aim spot behind the ball, and the ball will pop up and out softly and land with little roll. Before you put this shot into your bag of tricks, practice to help determine the force of swing needed for various distances.

Section 11:   314

A Rough Shot

Hitting from the rough around the green can be challenging, and there are several things to consider. First, choose a high-lofted club like a 60-degree sand wedge. This alone will be very helpful in getting the ball out. The next thing to do is place the ball in the middle or toward the back of your stance. This is critical to getting the club to cut through the grass. The last thing is to make a steeper take-away as if you are picking the club up. You want a steep angle to the ball much like a sand shot. Remember, hit through the shot to the finish and the ball will get up and out.

steep

PLAY BALL BACK

315

MASTER·STROKES

Use Extra Loft When You're In A Rough Neighborhood

Hitting out of the rough is tough enough, but if you have lost some club-head speed, the rough is even more challenging. When your ball is nestled down, the grass will wrap around the club's hosel at impact. This slows the club down tremendously and closes the clubface so that there's not enough loft on the club to get the ball out. The solution is that when you see you are in deep trouble, assess the lie, then choose an iron that has a loft two clubs higher than you think you would normally need. If you think you can get out with an 8-iron, use a wedge instead. Your ball will come out easier at a lower trajectory, with more roll than usual. You'll be pleasantly surprised with the results.

Roughing It

As an amateur, you might get a little more anxious when you end up in the rough. You're thinking you have to swing harder to compensate for lost strength. Bad plan. Swinging harder and trying to muscle the ball out of the tall grass results in an incorrect early release. This produces a low point behind the ball, putting lots of grass between the clubhead and the ball. Your main goal when hitting out of the rough is to minimize grass between your clubhead and the ball at impact. The correct approach is to play the ball back in your stance and open your clubface slightly. Swing with your normal rhythm, and wait for your club to accelerate at the ball. By correctly maintaining the angle between your wrist and clubshaft, your swing will bottom out at the ball and will lead to solid contact.

MASTER·STROKES

U.S. Open Survival

If you find yourself in heavy rough like the
players at the U.S. Open, you will need to
make a few adjustments to help you
survive. If you don't, the deep grass
will wrap up your clubhead before
impact, leaving your ball still in
deep trouble after your stroke.
First, position the ball way back
in your stance off the inside of your
rear foot, with most of your weight on
your front foot. Using this setup allows you
to swing on a much steeper arc than normal
and brings the clubhead down sharply on the
ball, which helps avoid much of the
grass that would get
between the clubhead and
ball. Because you are
swinging down so sharply,
let the ground stop your
follow-through shortly after
impact. Finally, use plenty of
loft for this shot – never select
anything less than a 7-iron.

Section 11: 318

MASTER·STROKES

Taming The High Rough

The best way to handle the high rough is not to get into it. However, the best players in the world find themselves buried in the rough from time to time. Here's how they escape. Play the ball back in your stance. The worse the rough, the farther back you need to play the ball. This encourages a quick pickup of the club in the beginning of the backswing. Aim 10 yards right of your target, as you will tend to pull these shots as the thick grass will do its best to close the clubface at impact. Finally, never use long irons here. You will have trouble getting the clubhead down into the ball. You don't want a shallow approach. Favor the short and mid irons.

LIGHTLY OPEN FACE

PLAY BALL BACK

AIM RIGHT

Problem Shots

NOT Easy Street!

You just hit your tee shot and it's heading a little to the right. You watch as it rolls off the fairway and comes to rest on the right side of a cart path. It's not the end of the world, as you're entitled to relief from the path without penalty. However, you must drop the ball within one club length to the nearest point of relief. In this case, you would need to drop to the right of the path. Normally, not much of a problem, but in this situation it would put your ball in the deep rough, making it much more likely you would hit the towering pine trees in front of you on your next shot. Now you're in more trouble? Not necessarily. Keep in mind that while taking a drop is allowed, you don't have to. You could opt to play the ball as it lies. If you're a player, you just might want to see if you can cleanly pick the ball off the cart path. Use your same swing and stance. Don't try to lift the ball, and avoid hitting down – you'll probably hit the path and injure yourself. You must have the club perfectly level through impact. With a fairway wood, contact the equator; with an iron, contact the ball a bit below the equator. This is an extremely difficult shot, so good luck.

Divot Dilemma

Nice drive! You just hit a sweet drive right on the screws. You watch your ball sail down the middle of the fairway, land and take a nice roll. You can't wait to hit your second shot, but as you come up to your ball, you find it sitting in a divot hole. Not good, but this doesn't mean you have to give up a stroke. You can hit the green by making some adjustments. First, take one club stronger than normal (example: a 6-iron versus a 7-iron). Second, choke down at least 1 inch on your grip – this automatically gives you a narrower swing arc and more control. Third, position the ball farther back, closer to your stance center. Fourth, keep more weight than normal on your left or front leg. Fifth, make an upright backswing, then swing down sharply into the back of the ball. This steep contact will give you an abbreviated, "punch"-type finish. The ball will come out lower than normal, so if there is room, try to land the ball short of the green and run the ball up.

MASTER·STROKES

Precise Pine Punch

We have all seen Tiger escape the woods with some incredibly powerful shots off pine needles. To pull off this recovery shot, seniors don't have to be as strong as Tiger. It's not that difficult to execute, with a few adjustments. Address the ball with 75 percent of your weight on your front foot. Move the ball back about 4 inches, just behind center of your stance. This deflofts your club, so use one club shorter than normal (9-iron instead of 8-iron). To stay in balance on the slippery needles, limit your backswing to three-quarter length with limited weight shift. You must catch the ball first with a descending blow and finish low, with the clubface pointing to the target. The ball will come out low, keeping it under any branches, but it will have much more backspin than you'd get from normal rough.

3/4

75%

MASTER·STROKES

Avoid A Big Number

The casual golfer most likely isn't driving the ball 300 yards. He might not carry his 7-iron 160 yards up and over the pine trees. However, if you do play regularly, without a doubt you have learned from experience that when you are in trouble, you need to be smart and try to get out of trouble in one stroke! From here on in, abide by this simple rule: Anytime you are in jail, get out immediately in the simplest manner possible. Let the inexperienced player try the hero shot. Watch him write the big number on his scorecard. You have learned to avoid the big number. Take the sure bet rather than the high-risk, impossible shot and play out of trouble – take the easy way out! You see big-enough numbers on your birthday card.

WISER→

R. YOUNGER

323

Problem Shots

Hazardous To Your Score Card

Not all hazards are sand traps or water. There are other areas on the course that can be marked as hazards, such as wetlands. Let's say your ball has landed in a hazard like this, but you would be able to hit your shot and escape. This would avoid taking a drop outside of the hazard area and the penalty stroke that goes with it. But you must remember you cannot ground your club in all hazard areas before hitting your shot. This includes practice swings where your club touches the ground. If you forget, you will incur a one-stroke penalty for each practice swing in which your club makes contact with the surface. The solution is to back out of the margin of the hazard, get the feel of the swing needed through practice swings, then step back in and hit your shot.

The Lay-up Shot

Let's assume you have 170 yards to the water and you normally hit your 5-iron that distance. Don't choose the 5-iron and tell yourself that you will just ease up on the club. You will tend to hold back so much that you will probably decelerate through impact, leaving the clubface open at impact, and hit a big slice or fat shot. The way to lay up is to figure out the distance to the water, pick an area of grass 10 to 20 yards in front of the water and select the club that you hit that distance with a free swing. Be careful not to get close enough that your ball will hit a hard patch or downslope and go into the drink.

325

Davy Jones Golf

Water hazards make you uptight? Join the crowd. Most recreational golfers share your fear. Here's a simple strategy to help ease your nerves. Don't simply calculate the distance of your shot and select a club that, if hit perfectly, will give you that distance. What are the odds of hitting a perfect shot?

We already admitted that we all get a little tight when carrying water. And what's the price you'll pay if you go swimming?

Let's say your lie and distance would normally have you reaching for your wedge. You'd probably be wiser to choose your 8-iron. If you hit it sweet and end up a little long, you shouldn't have a difficult recovery and can walk to the next tee with a par. The knowledge that you have plenty of club allows you to make a relaxed swing. This reduces your chance of a mishit that sends your ball to a watery grave.

'Yo! Fuhgeddaboudit!'

Water holes strike fear into many amateurs. Approach shots or tee shots that must carry over water suddenly find amateurs having all kinds of trouble, even if the carry is one they would normally make with no problem. When facing a scary water carry, here's a trick to ease your mind. Stand behind the ball, looking at the target. Now dream up a beautiful green fairway and imagine it lies between you and the target. Step up to the ball and go through your regular routine without hesitation, all the while keeping the fairway image in mind. Then take your normal, relaxed swing. You'll find success with this approach, which will relax you. Greatly reduce your fear of water carry shots and replace it with confidence.

327

Problem Shots

Splish Splash, Don't Take A Bath

One of the most memorable and rewarding shots you can hit is a splash shot out of a water hazard. Here's how to play it and save that penalty drop. First, make certain half of the ball is visible above the water. If it's totally submerged, you have no shot. Use a pitching wedge. The sand wedge's thick flange creates too much friction against the water. If you can get a stance, play the ball in the middle of your stance. Pick the club up abruptly, and give a good whack into the water about two inches behind the ball. Don't try to follow through, and don't be shy. Hit hard, as you don't want to leave it in the water. And be prepared to get a bit wet and muddy!

PITCHING WEDGE

2" BEHIND

MUST HAVE HALF OF BALL SHOWING

OPEN FACE BALL BACK IN STANCE

April Showers Can Bring High Scores

As spring inches closer, many golfers who have been stuck in the brutal winter are itching to get out there.

But remember, with the spring comes rain. Playing in wet conditions affects everyone's game, but players who don't hit the ball very far struggle more when the course is wet.

The lower-flying shots, which would normally land short but have added roll, will instead stop quickly in wet grass. This means you have to try to carry your shots as far as possible in the air.

So think of switching out some of the clubs in your bag. You should be hitting a 3-wood off the tee instead of a driver. Next replace your longest iron (3-iron?) with a 7-wood or 9-wood. Final adjustment? Plan your approach shots to land all the way up to the flag. Making these strategic adjustments due to the conditions will give you your best chance to stay competitive in "April showers."

DRIVER →

3 IRON →

← 3 WOOD

← 7 WOOD

329

Get Some Air In The Rain

Rainy-day golf doesn't simply mean wearing rain gear. It also means making adjustments to your swing, shot-making approach and equipment. The ball stops quickly in wet grass, with very little roll. This is especially tough on players who lack distance and depend on roll.

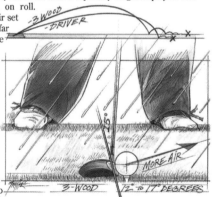

They need to switch out their set for clubs that will carry as far as possible in the air. Take your driver out of your bag and replace it with a 3-wood. If your longest iron is a 4-iron, consider taking it out and replacing it with a 7-wood or a 9-wood instead. Remember, your ball won't roll, so aim all your approach shots to land nearly all the way to the flag. Be aware not to press in the rain or swing faster. If you want to get the shot over with so you can get back into the cart or under the umbrella, you're only rushing to a more miserable day of golf, with a disastrous score card.

MASTER·STROKES

Play It Straight

It's harder to draw or fade the ball when it's wet. On rainy days, moisture will get between the clubface and golf ball at impact, giving you less grip on the ball compared with dry conditions. This causes your shots to carry less backspin and less sidespin, making it difficult to "shape" your shots. If you try to draw your shot, it will most likely hang out to the right, and a shot you're trying to fade will likely stay left of the target. So the sensible game plan for playing in the rain is to keep it simple. Play it straight and aim directly for your target in the fairway or the green. Also, remember that you will get less roll, so adjust your club selection.

Flight Control

Windy days make approach shots difficult. For example, a right-to-left crosswind will push a straight shot off line to the left in flight, and the ball will bounce and roll farther left upon landing. These conditions make it hard to hold the green, never mind getting the ball close to the pin.

The way to fight crosswinds is to hit a draw or a fade (a fade against a right-to-left wind, and a draw against a left-to-right wind). If you can shape your shots, do so; if not, this is another reason to learn.

The sidespin of these shots going against the wind will counteract the wind, so the shot has a chance of holding its line. A shot that "fights" the crosswind will also stop much more quickly upon landing.

Final tip: When hitting a draw or a fade into a crosswind, use one club longer than normal.

MASTER·STROKES

CUT A NEW DEAL

You're a veteran – you should be able to renegotiate a better deal for yourself on cold, wet and windy spring days. You're understandably rusty from a long, tough winter. So when the weather is nasty, ease up on what is "par for the course." Too many seniors expect too much. In the middle of a round that isn't going well, they often get frustrated, and all the wheels fall off. Disastrous rounds like this can get the whole season heading in the wrong direction. Keep things in perspective, and set a realistic goal. Realize that under these conditions, a good score for you might be an extra stroke for each hole. Take the pressure off by adjusting your own personal par for the course. You'll enjoy the game more and be in a better mind-set for a great season.

Problem Shots

MASTER·STROKES

Be A Slowpoke

It's best to keep it under 55 when it's under 55. In other words, NO SPEEDING! Everyone has a tendency to swing faster than normal when it's cold out. When you're all bundled up and not as loose, it's easy to make an all-arms swing with little body turn. This results in a faster swing motion that generates little power. Of course, this is more harmful to players who are already less supple and more likely to be making a fast, all-arms swing in cold weather. The way to combat the cold-weather effects is to make a swing that literally feels like it's in slow motion. It won't actually be as slow as it feels, but this consciously slower swing will give your upper torso some extra time to turn more fully on the backswing. This, in turn, will allow you to use your torso to turn smoothly through the impact zone, giving you maximum power in cold conditions.

Section 11:

334

Low, Cold Blow

Golf shots will fly differently in different air temperatures. You won't be able to carry the ball as far or as high in very cold weather. So, realize you can't play your summer game in the winter – "you can't fight Mother Nature." Instead, play smart and adjust for the cold air. If a shot calls for a 5-iron in warm weather, drop down to a 4-iron. Play for a shot that will fly lower and land a little short of the green and then run up on to it. Don't try to overpower shots in cold conditions. Overswinging only leads to a frustrating round filled with mishits and possible injury in the cold. So "chill out" and go low so you can enjoy carding a low score when you come in from the cold.

You Never Know

Even after years of playing many rounds of golf, you still never know what kind of unusual shot you might come across. It could be a left-handed shot for a righty, a ball in a bunker where you must stand outside and hit a ball way below your feet, or a ball on a clump of grass above your feet while you're in a water hazard. The point is, you never know. What you should know is, don't try it until you've practiced it. So when you do face a situation where it requires a very odd swing, the best advice is to not try a full shot unless you have practiced it before. If you haven't "felt" the swing that's needed, you will most likely mishit the shot, getting yourself into more trouble, or even "whiff" it. The next thing you know, the wheels are falling off your round. Instead, play a safe chip into the fairway, setting yourself up for a comfortable next shot, or take an unplayable-lie penalty, if necessary. In the future, practice different stances and grips for unusual shots if you want to be more ready for the unexpected.

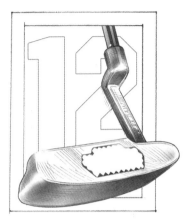

SECTION 12:
Putting

As the least physically demanding aspect of golf, putting offers the chance for golfers of all ages and skill levels to excel. Putting is not, however, without its challenges and frustrations. The tips in this chapter will help you to recognize, analyze and overcome the most common and vexing of them to become a better putter—and a much better golfer in the process.

CONTENTS

Putting 101

Putting is very personal. In the history of the game, we have seen many great players use many different styles. That said, here are some basics: **HEAD STILL** Set up square or maybe a little open to the ball. Play the ball slightly inside your left heel, with your eyes directly over it and parallel to the target line. Keep your hands in line with the ball, and set your putter face at a right angle to the hole. For your basic stroke on putts under 15 feet, **LIGHT GRIP** make a pendulum-type backswing, controlling the action with the triangle formed by your arms and shoulders. The triangle stays intact back and through, feeling as if you are rocking your shoulders or making the stroke with the muscles in your upper back.

On this length stroke or shorter, the putter face should stay square to the target. On longer putts, the face should swing slightly inside the target line on a natural arc. **PUTT FROM SHOULDERS** Make your stroke as rhythmic as possible; tension is a killer when putting. It's OK to have the backswing and follow-through equal in length, but if not, it's best to have the follow-through shorter, with a "hit and hold" sensation. Watch film of Ben Crenshaw, Gary Player or Brad Faxon.

Read It And Reap

You can reap the benefits of reading a green way before you get on it to make your putt.

If you're playing a hilly course, you can start "reading" the green as you approach it. Take advantage by observing the fall of the land as you walk toward the green. Say it slopes sharply to the right. If so, even if the green appears to be flat when you're on it, the odds are that it will slope a bit to the right.

Confirm this point by trying a few practice putts on a green that also lies in a sharply sloping area. You'll find that the green does have more break than you thought, in the direction of the general lay of the land.

341

Intel Report

You should always pay attention when your opponent is putting. There is valuable information that could be the difference between a birdie and a bogey. Here is an example: Your opponent is away, looking at a 25-footer. You're 15 feet away but roughly on the same line, so you mark your ball. Watch the roll of the opponent's ball very closely as it reaches the area where you will putt from until it reaches the hole. The ball might break a little more or a little less than you would have thought beforehand. It also could surprise you by pulling up short, indicating that the green is slower than you thought, or by running way past, indicating it's fast. Use this free intel to your advantage.

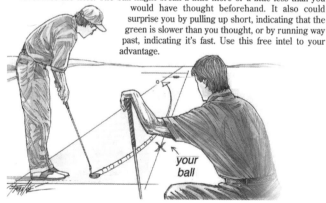

your
ball

Get a Grip

The purpose of the putting grip is to stabilize the hands and prevent excess hinging at the wrist. The standard putting grip is the "reverse overlap." It is formed by laying the club across the palm of the left hand, with the handle running diagonally from the base of the forefinger along the heel pad or the lifeline between the heel and thumb pads. The "V" formed by the thumb and forefinger of the left hand points to the left shoulder. All four fingers and thumb of the right hand go on the handle, with the "V" formed by the thumb and forefinger pointing to the right shoulder. The forefinger of the left hand overlaps the fingers of the right.

Putting

MASTER·STROKES

Cross Over To The Dark Side

At one point, your putting was OK. Now, you're struggling. Try this. Years ago, the cross-handed putting (left hand low for right-handers) grip was seen as a refuge, or last-ditch effort, to fix a struggling stroke. However, in present-day golf instruction it has become much more than that. Cross-handed putting actually has an advantage over traditional putting in one very important way. It puts the left hand (for right-handers) in a strong, leading position. This prevents the right hand from taking over and having the left wrist break down during the stroke. For any golfer, young or old, the cross-handed putting stroke can be a great asset on fast, undulating greens. Try it for more consistency.

REVERSE HANDS, LEFT HAND LOW

Stand Tall

The casual golfer might have the time to practice putting, but he maybe just doesn't have the back for it. This is especially true if your style is bent over like Jack Nicklaus as opposed to Tiger Woods' straight-up stance. We know putting well takes practice time. By practicing for an hour bent over, you run the risk of not being able to play the next day due to back pain. Consider giving your old back a break. In addition, it might be a good idea to get a longer putter. You'll get used to it, and your back will thank you for it.

GIVE YOUR BACK A BREAK

FRANKE

Putting

MASTER·STROKES

Pendulum Putting

The putting stroke is like a pendulum, swinging back and through. This is a one-piece triangle of the arms and shoulders that stays intact during putting, rhythmically rocking equally through the backstroke and follow-through.

You should feel as if you're simply rocking your shoulders, or even that you're making the stroke with the muscles in your upper back. Your shoulders should act as a teeter-totter. This keeps the triangle solidly intact and prevents the grip end from moving too far, which is what you want. It makes the stroke as simple and repetitive as possible.

An added thought to go with this "keep it simple" basic putting tip is to hum yourself a tune while going through your putting routine and stroke. Many Tour pros do this to help them relax. A simple and relaxed stroke will definitely have you sinking more putts.

Firm Up, Soft Down

Many golfers fail to hit their uphill putts hard enough, leaving the ball short. Or they miss because they didn't hit it firm enough into the slope to hold the intended line. On the other hand, they will hit their downhill putts too firmly, without any touch, so if the putt misses, it zips well past the hole.

Here's an easy-to-remember rule for golfers having trouble on sloping greens: "Firm up, soft down."

On uphill putts, stroke firmly enough so that the ball hits the back of the cup lightly before dropping in. Even if you miss, since it's rolling uphill, the ball will stop just past. On downhillers, try to make the ball drop just over the front lip without touching the back of the hole. This way, should you miss, the ball will still stop within tap-in distance.

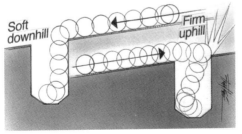

Soft downhill   Firm uphill

Slow Greens

All of us encounter very slow greens from time to time. It might be after several days of inclement weather when the greens could not be cut. This is especially troublesome for those golfers whose putting stroke has become uncertain or a little weak. Here are a few tips to help you to putt better on slow greens. First, add wrist action. Allow your hands to set your wrists in the backstroke. Then release the putter head through the ball. Second, accelerate the putter head through impact. Imagine a small nail in the back of the ball. Hit that nail dead center. These adjustments should result in a stronger, firmer putting stroke.

Set Wrist

ACCELERATE

Fast And Downhill Putts – Be On Your Toe

The next time you face one of those slick and fast downhill putts that has "THREE-PUTT" written all over it, try this trick that pro golfers have been using for years. Align the ball and stroke the putt off the toe end of the putter face. That's right, intentionally miss the sweet spot of the putter, and roll the putt off the toe. The toe end of the putter is the weakest part of the putter face and will "deaden" or soften impact substantially. This will take some speed off your putt. This technique greatly lessens the chance of running your ball way past the hole, leaving you a long, aggravated return putt. But be careful not to let your face twist open when you do make contact on the toe – an open face will make your ball miss right.

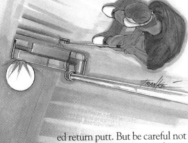

MASTER·STROKES

Gain The Feel Of A Pro

To achieve better feel, practice putting on the green while looking at the target. Imagine how hard you must strike the ball to make it roll the correct distance. By shifting your attention to the hole rather than focusing on the ball or the putter, you'll make a smoother, less mechanical stroke and greatly improve your touch.

MASTER·STROKES

Lighten Up

This putting tip is so simple but so incredibly effective. Hold your putter as light as you possibly can without it slipping from your hands. A tight grip is a tension grip.

TENSION KILLS! You know it – tension ruins all athletic movement. It robs you of your natural instinctive "feel." Hold the putter in the softest, most gentle grip you can. You'll find touch you never knew you had. Line and speed also will improve. You'll be dropping putts all over the place. Your friends won't know who you are. Show them your name on your low score card.

Light & Soft

Putting

Hum A Tune

I spent a good amount of time with golf legend Sam Snead. Under pressure, Sam, who played very well as a senior, would whistle a tune under his breath to relax. Tension will kill your putting stroke – you lose all your "feel."

Obviously, it worked well enough for Sam to hold the all-time PGA Tour record of 82 official victories. You might do well humming a melody between shots or even over a must-make putt. This little trick can really improve tempo.

Relax!

Lose that muscle tension and let your stroke flow!

Stop 'Puttering' Around

Amateurs sometimes get too "antsy," with too much nervous movement in their putting stroke with their hands and wrists. A good choice of stroke type for seniors is one that relies only on the large muscles, with the upper arms and shoulders providing the power. This type is the most reliable and repetitive. Set up to putt with your arms relatively straight, and with your hands, arms and shoulders forming a triangle. Use your upper arms and shoulders to move this one-piece triangle away from and back through the ball. All your quiet hands and wrists are doing is holding the club. This will give you a true and consistent roll.

Don't Forget When It's Wet

The odds are that due to spring rains, you'll be putting on some wet greens to start the season. It doesn't matter if the wet green is from April showers or early-morning dew. It's important to remember that your ball will not break as much on a wet putting surface. Wet conditions will greatly minimize the amount a putt can break. Water in the grass will build up resistance to the ball, reducing its speed. More significantly, the water that gets into the ball's dimples will not allow it to break as it would on a dry green. Taking this fact into account, you must play less break. Make sure you spend some extra time on the practice green to help figure out how much adjustment you need to make to help you sink your putts on wet greens.

A Grain Of Truth

On many putting surfaces, particularly Bermuda greens in warm climates, the grass leans in one direction. This type of grass is said to have a "grain," and grain is a big factor in your overall read of the putt. Here's a tip to help you read the grain. Look directly down at the cup, taking note of the edges. If on one side of the cup the grass looks ruffled, while the opposite side is neat and clean, the grain is growing from the ruffled side toward the clean side.

So if you're putting with the ruffled side at the rear of the cup, the putt is "into" the grain, and you must stroke more firmly. If the clean side is at the rear, you are putting "with" the grain, and the ball will roll a bit farther than normal. If the ruffled grass is on either side of the cup, plan for the putt to break away from that side a little more than you'd think.

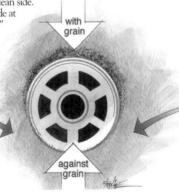

355 **Putting**

MASTER·STROKES

Go Pro

When making a putt, casual golfers should commit to favoring the high side, better known as the "pro" side. This is especially true after all the years of missing shots on the low side of the hole (statistically, most missed putts are on the low side). Unfortunately, you'd probably agree with this, bringing back some unpleasant memories.

So let's get that old dog learning some new tricks. From now on, after reading your putt and identifying the break, aim for the high side. Don't be afraid to put more break into every putt you hit. Play more aggressively on every putt you see. Play like a pro. You will make more putts, and that will definitely improve your score.

Section 12:

Double Trouble

Longer putts will sometimes travel over the green by first breaking one way, then the other. How do you judge the line of these double breakers accurately? With your brain along with your eyes.

Let's say you're facing a 35-foot putt. For 15 feet, it breaks right to left. Then it flattens out for 5 feet, and the remaining distance breaks left to right. In a case like this, you might assume that the two breaks cancel each other out, so you should start the ball straight to the hole. You must not forget that the ball will break more as it slows down. In this scenario, it will break more to the right as it approaches the hole and is slowing down. You would aim this putt slightly left of the hole.

LESS SPEED
MORE BREAK

MORE SPEED
LESS BREAK

15'

15'

FRANKE

Lag Putting

Before you step up into the first tee box for your next round of golf, spend an extra 10 minutes on the putting green. Use these 10 minutes to focus on lag putting, and concentrate on distance control only. Use only one ball, and hit putts of more than 30 feet. Putt to a hole or any other target, such as a tee placed at the edge of the green. Do not finish out. I'd rather you hit long putt after long putt. By going back and forth across the putting green, you will practice all types of slopes while sharpening your touch. Take this "feel" to the course with you. Now you can tee off. This more thorough practice will usually translate into lower scores.

Section 12:

358

An Easy Line Up

Poor aim, rather than an errant stroke, is the main cause of golfers missing putts.

Here's a simple tip you should make a habit for every single putt: After you've determined the starting line of the putt, place your ball so that the label lies directly along that line. Then simply set your putter blade down so that it is at a perfect right angle to the ball's label. You can visually see that you're beautifully and precisely squared to the target line. Now you can make a nice, relaxed, confident stroke and listen for the ball falling into the cup.

TARGET LINE

LABEL

Putt Yourself In A Head Lock!

We have pointed out that some head movement is necessary in order to have an athletic, fluid golf swing. This is not true while putting. If your head is moving during your putting stroke, you are not making many putts. When your head moves, your upper body and arms move with it. This excess movement means the blade of the putter will not impact the ball as precisely as planned. It doesn't take much head movement to throw the blade off enough to affect the path of the ball by an inch or two, the difference between a make and a miss.

As you settle in over the ball, imagine a large vise being lightly tightened against your temples, fixing your head's position in space. Make your stroke with your head locked in that vise. Never look up until you hear your putt fall into the cup.

MASTER·STROKES

Wide When Windy

Believe it or not, even the slightest body movement during the stroke can alter the angle of the putter face enough to send the putt off line. It doesn't take much. It's also harder than you realize to stay perfectly still if you're playing in windy conditions. So you need to shore yourself up to help withstand the wind.

Here's a simple but rock-solid tip on a blustery day.

Widen your putting stance by spreading your feet 6 to 8 inches wider than normal. A wider base is more stable and lowers your body mass to the ground.

This minor adjustment increases your ability to keep still during your stroke. You'll hear more putts drop in the breeze.

6 TO 8"
WIDER

Putting

Sweet Putting

There are many factors involved in good putting: reading the green correctly, using proper alignment, having good aim and making a smooth, rhythmic stroke. These are all important, but the most important element is hitting the ball on the putter's "sweet spot," or the center of percussion. This very basic need often is overlooked or taken for granted by unknowing amateurs and seniors. Here's how to find it: While holding your putter vertically, slowly and firmly tap the face with a tee. Take note of how the putter is rebounding from your taps. What you are looking for is the spot that rebounds straight back without vibration. Mark this spot, if needed. Note: Some manufacturers have graphics on the top of their putters. This is not always the center of percussion. Once you discover your sweet spot, make it your business to hit it every time you putt so you get the truest possible roll. Go drain some putts! Sweet!

Keep Level-Headed

We're talking about your putter head. Many golfers tend to stroke their putts with a downward jabbing motion. This abrupt, steep type of stroke drives the ball into the putting surface, causing it to bounce upward instead of getting off to a smooth end-over-end roll. To avoid this erratic, unpredictable roll you must concentrate on keeping your stroke as level and low to the ground as possible. To help you do this, practice this drill. Lay down at least a 12-inch ruler just outside the toe of your putter, alongside the ball line. Attempt a stroke in which the bottom of the putter blade nearly brushes the grass for 6 inches on either side of the ball's position. That is 6 inches behind the ball on the backstroke to 6 inches past the ball on the follow-through. This low, level stroke will give you a sweet end-over-end roll for "true" accurate putting.

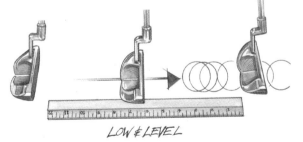

LOW & LEVEL

363   **Putting**

MASTER·STROKES

-1,2, ROLL 'H!

DON'T FREEZE

Take Two Looks And Let It Roll

I have seen more putts missed due to the golfer freezing over the golf ball while reviewing a hundred different putting-stroke thoughts in his head. It's as though he has forgotten there is a hole and the goal is to roll the ball into it. Used to be simple, right? The goal isn't to make a perfect stroke. Save that quest for practice. Next time you play, just get into your setup, get comfortable and take two looks at the hole. Then, don't wait, don't think, just roll the ball into the hole. That's the goal.

So stop overthinking and start stroking. Got it?

Section 12:

Piston Stroke

Inconsistent putting is very often caused by a "flippy" left wrist breaking down through impact. A unique way to help eliminate left-wrist breakdown is "Pop Piston Putting."

At address, set your right wrist in a bent-backward position so your right hand and your right forearm form a distinct angle. After your backstroke, push your right hand and the club together toward the target with a solid, pistonlike motion. Make sure that the angle of your right wrist never changes. Your left wrist will automatically remain firm and, importantly, in front of the blade at impact because of this pistonlike motion of the right hand. This stroke will give your putts a level, solid and consistent hit.

MASTER·STROKES

Being The Same Is 'Kool'

Many golfers get nervous over putts, particularly short- to middle-distance putts they need to score well or "make par." A nervous stroke is a shaky, erratic stroke.

The best way to make a "nerveless" stroke is to make the stroke part of a routine. It's not so important what movements you make. It's more important to set a pre-stroke routine that flows smoothly into the stroke itself. For example, you might set the blade behind the ball, look from ball to hole once or twice, make a slight forward press of your hands toward the target and then go. The key is to make these movements the same way every time, then immediately continue to flow into the stroke itself. Developing a rock-solid routine will give you a tension-free, confident stroke, making your putting stroke "automatic."

True Hole Center

What would you say if someone asked you which part of the hole you were aiming for when you were putting? My guess is you'd answer, "The center, of course." Obvious answer, but keep in mind that on sharply breaking putts, the "true hole center" changes. It is not the front center in relation to where you are starting your putt; it is the front center in relation to the roll of the putt as it breaks toward the hole. On a putt that breaks sharply right-to-left, you should be aiming for a spot on the lip to the right of the front center, therefore increasing your odds for the ball to go in. And if the putt breaks sharply left-to-right, you should be aiming to try to drop the ball over the lip at a spot to the left of the front center. This approach will give you a much greater chance of dropping impressive, sharp-breaking putts.

Short-Putting Imagery

When you really need to get a short putt into the hole, imagery becomes crucial. The more vivid the mental picture, the better you will focus on the positive. This is especially true with those who might be more susceptible to self-doubt and tension, leading to "jitters" on these short putts. One image that has worked very well in my teaching is that of a small ditch. This ditch runs from under your ball into the center of the hole. Then strike that short putt with total confidence. The ball cannot roll out of the ditch. It can only go in the hole.